GODS AND GODDESSES

GODS AND GODDESSES

A Treasury of Deities and Tales from World Mythology

General Editor
ELIZABETH HALLAM

MACMILLAN • U.S.A.

MACMILLAN

A Simon & Schuster Macmillan Company

1633 Broadway

New York, NY 10019–6785

Library of Congress Cataloging-in-Publication Data
Gods & goddesses : a treasury of deities and tales from world
mythology / Elizabeth Hallam, general editor.
p.   cm.
Includes bibliographical references.
ISBN 0-02-861421-6
1. Gods.   2. Goddesses.   3. Mythology.   I. Hallam. Elizabeth M.
BL473.G55   1996   96-20795
291.2'11—dc20   CIP
10 9 8 7 6 5 4 3 2 1

AN EDDISON·SADD EDITION
Edited, designed, and produced by
Eddison Sadd Editions Limited
St Chad's House
148 King's Cross Road
London WC1X 9DH

Phototypeset in Venetian 301 BT using QuarkXPress on Apple Macintosh
Origination by Columbia Overseas Marketing, Singapore
Printed by Dai Nippon Printing Company, Hong Kong

CONTENTS

INTRODUCTION

─────────────── ✳ ───────────────

From the dawn of history, men and women have revered a vast pantheon of gods and goddesses, divine beings who epitomize the mysteries of the universe and who can be worshipped, placated, and invoked to fulfill humankind's deep-felt need for an other-worldly dimension to everyday life. And as civilizations and cultures developed across the globe, each of them created its own theology, mythology, and religious rituals with its own principles and doctrines.

Nevertheless, the shared beliefs of these numerous and diverse religions are as striking as the differences between them: their deities have enormous power over the forces of nature, the animal world, and human beings. And they provide answers to questions about the physical and spiritual world that have tantalized and perplexed men and women through the millennia.

The theme of a supreme creator deity runs through all of them. Most, too, have gods and goddesses of the sun, of the moon and nature, of earth, sea, and sky, of vegetation, of the fertility of the soil and the fecundity of humankind, of love, marriage, and mother-hood. In many, the home and household have their deities, as do arts and crafts, and the

more abstract qualities and principles of truth, knowledge, justice, and peace. There are also deities of war, dark gods of the underworld and black magic, and malevolent and trickster gods who are regarded as being responsible for human misfortunes and misery.

This book draws together the gods and god-desses who exemplify these themes and, to emphasize the importance of their roles in the daily lives of their devotees, is arranged by the deities' spheres of influence. Its approach is neither that of comparative religion nor a study of mythology; it is not written from the standpoint of any religion and, in keeping with modern scholarship, makes no value judgments. Rather, *Gods and Goddesses* focuses on the deities themselves and their "human" characteristics, their origins and the legends about them, the rites in their honor, and their

─────────────── ✳ ───────────────

Eros, the Greek god of love, is shown here in his romantic form as a chubby, winged infant, armed with the bow and arrow with which he pierces the hearts of men. He was originally a primeval god who issued from chaos, and represented the force of attraction that held the world together and ensured the continuation of the species.

appearance and attributes. Many of them have multiple functions that can seem complex and contradictory, and these are explained in the text and appear in the index; but the selection of their main functions is well-supported in authoritative sources (*see Bibliography page 178*).

The deities have been chosen from religions and cultures that differ in time and location. Among the most ancient are the gods and goddesses of Egypt, whose study enables us to gain a greater understanding of the world view held by such enduringly popular figures as the pharaohs Rameses II and Tutankhamen. Some key figures in the Egyptian pantheon were Osiris, god of the underworld, his consort and devoted widow Isis, goddess of magic, and Re, the sun god; on a more domestic level the much-revered cat goddess Bastet epitomized pleasure and sensuality.

Some Egyptian ideas fed through into the worship of the ancient Greeks, who in their turn profoundly influenced the religion of Rome. The Greek myths circulated in many different versions, most notably the epics of Homer which are still widely read. Zeus, the all-powerful, had many consorts both divine and human, from Hera, his wife and sister, and Demeter, goddess of fruitfulness, to Thetis, a nymph of the sea. Other notable figures in the Greek pantheon included Dionysos, god of fertility, wine, and ecstasy; Ares, god of war and violence; Aphrodite, goddess of love; and Hades, dark king of the underworld. These all had their equivalents in the religion of Rome; but the Romans also had their own deities like Janus, god of gateways and beginnings, and the Lares and Penates, guardians of the home. In addition, they equated many of the local gods in the lands they conquered with their own deities.

An example is the Celtic Lug, god of all skills, whom the Romans saw as the equivalent of their messenger god Mercury.

The Celts' deities were more obscure and less consistent in their attributes than those of classical Greece and Rome. Nevertheless, the Dagda, lord of all knowledge, Epona, goddess of the underworld, and Cernunnos, the antlered god of virility, were widely worshipped in Celtic northern Europe, and traces still remain in the folklore and works of art of regions settled by the Celts.

The northern peoples of Germany and Scandinavia produced two races of gods—the Vanir and the Aesir, who were later syncretized—and a rich mythological heritage overshadowed by the prospect of Ragnarok, the last great battle when the gods of light will be overwhelmed by the forces of evil; their deities, like Odin, ruler of heaven, Thor, god of thunder, and Freya, goddess of sex, were strong, powerful, lusty, and warlike. This mythology inspired stirring tales over subsequent centuries.

The gods and goddesses of the Inuit of the Arctic region of North America reflect a harsh, northern environment and the dependency of its people on the wild creatures of the sea over whom the watery goddess Sedna rules. Myths and rituals involving the animal kingdom are also a widespread and key element in the religions of the native North American peoples: Coyote, the dangerous quicksilver trickster, is found across the continent, as are the Thunderbirds, creators of storms. The sun, also, is ubiquitous—sun dances are a continuing practice—and has many different manifestations such as Tsohanoai, the Navajo sun bearer.

The gods and religious practices of the

Central American native peoples—the Maya, Toltecs and Aztecs—survive rarely and only in attenuated forms. The Spanish conquistadors and the missionaries who followed them were determined to stamp out the cults of deities such as Huitzilopochtli, god of war and the sun, the devouring earth goddess Coatlicue, and Tezcatlipoca, sorcerer god of the smoking mirror, with their focus on human sacrifice—while removing the gold and silver that was a prominent feature in their worship. The same fate befell South American deities like Viracocha, the Inca lord of the world, to whom small girls were sacrificed on Andean mountaintops.

Despite the great cultural diversity of Africa, there is a major unifying theme—the worship of one great creator god—in all its religions, some of which have been tenaciously preserved. The Zulu supreme creator god Unkulunkulu is appropriately strong and war-like; in Zaire, Nzambi, the deity of the sun, is omniscient, kind, and caring toward the poor. On the other side of the world, in Oceania, the best-known god is the trickster-hero Maui, who flouts convention and represents the triumph of the weak over the strong.

The richly textured, reflective religions of China, Japan, and India have evolved over the millennia, and they draw together many diverse traditions: Taoism, Confucianism, Shintoism, Hinduism, Buddhism. Chinese mythology stretches back over four thousand years with a pantheon that encompasses a great variety of deities, from the ancient and all-powerful Shang Di, to Kwan Yin, the compassionate goddess of motherhood who evolved from a male Indian bodhisattva (enlightened being), and the influential household deities Shou Lao and Ts'ai Shen.

Drawing on Shinto and Buddhist traditions, the Japanese look to Izanagi and Izanami as the primal couple from whom the earth originated. In India, Vishnu reigns supreme with his consort Lakshmi, patron of wives. Various human and animal figures represent his different incarnations or avatars, including the righteous Rama, hero of the epic *Ramayana*. Shiva is the terrible agent of destruction, but his elephant-headed son, Ganesha, brings good fortune and success to his devotees.

Fascinating for their variety and diversity, and equally intriguing for the themes that unite them, the gods and goddesses in this book reflect beliefs that have developed over many centuries—even millennia—of human existence. But despite their ancient roots, they, like many of thousands of others across the globe, are with us still—culturally in literature and art or as the deities of living religions, divine reminders of humankind's never-ending quest for spiritual enlightenment.

A NOTE ON SPELLING

The names of the deities in this book are spelled according to a variety of different conventions in different sources, and the main variations are indicated with each entry. Here, the main authority is A. Cotterell, *A Dictionary of World Mythology,* Oxford University Press, 1986. Other authorities have an asterisk in the Bibliography (*see page 178*). All the main versions of the names are given in the Index.

Elizabeth Hallam
London UK, July 1996

CHAPTER ONE

❋

SUPREME AND CREATOR GODS

CREATOR OF THE UNIVERSE

❋

ATUM
Egypt

Atum was a self-created deity, the first being to emerge from the dark and endless watery abyss that girdled the world before creation. A product of the energy and matter contained in this chaos, he created divine and human beings through loneliness: alone in the universe, he produced from his own semen Shu, the god of air, and Tefnut, the goddess of moisture. The brother and sister, curious about the primeval waters by which they were surrounded, went to explore them—and disappeared into their impenetrable darkness. Unable to bear his loss, Atum sent a fiery messenger to find his children. The tears of joy he shed on their return were the first human beings.

Atum is often called lord of Heliopolis—the major center of sun worship—and associated with another deity on the site, the sun god Re. As the creative principle of all life, Atum gave

ABOVE The ultimate source of pharaonic power, Atum wears the combined crowns of Lower and Upper Egypt.

OPPOSITE Vishnu, the supreme god of Hindu mythology, is surrounded by his avatars.

human beings their different colored skins, different climate, and lands. To Egypt he gave the Nile. Creatures sacred to Atum include the bull, lion, and lizard. The most significant is the snake, which stands for the inevitable cosmic holocaust that only Atum and Osiris will survive.

He is generally represented in human form and, as the source of the pharaoh's power, wears the double crown of Egypt—red for Lower Egypt, white for Upper Egypt—and carries a tall cross, the symbol of eternal life.

ALSO KNOWN AS: Tum, Tem, Atumu, Tumu, Atum-Re

✳

CREATOR OF ALL THINGS

✳

TANGAROA
Oceania (Polynesia)

The creator of all things, Tangaroa lived alone in a dark mussel shell long before the birth of the universe. When the earth and sky were separated, the sea covered everything, and Tangaroa, coming out of his shell, had to create the world with its natural features, the gods, and all living beings.

He was lord of the sea, fishes and reptiles, winds and air—even, according to some traditions, of plants and vegetation. He was also patron of housebuilders—the first house was said to have been built in heaven.

Tangaroa was as quarrelsome as he was busy. He could not forgive his brother Tane, the forest god, for having separated the sea and the sky, and maintained an ongoing war with him. Tane, with his wooden canoes, and fishhooks, and fishnets woven from wood fibers, was responsible for the killing of sea creatures. Tangaroa then retaliated by ordering the sea to swallow the canoes, the trees, the forests, the wooden houses and even, with its lapping waves, the shores and beaches.

Tangaroa is usually represented as a supreme god, creating other gods and human beings. His body, often hollow and containing several statuettes of idols, is studded with small carvings symbolizing his creations.

ALSO KNOWN AS: Kanaloa, Taaora

✳

✳

This wooden carving from the Polynesian island of Tubai represents Tangaroa in the process of creating other gods. According to Hawaiian legends, however, Tangaroa was an evil god, associated with sorcery and the underworld: his curse introduced death into the world.

✳

SUPREME CREATOR

✻

UNKULUNKULU
Africa (Zulu)

Supreme creator god of the Zulus of South Africa, Unkulunkulu created the universe, including all living things. He was himself the first man and was regarded as the great ancestor, or first Zulu.

In the beginning, when there was nothing but a vast swamp full of many-colored reeds, Unkulunkulu created himself from one of them. Then he broke off pairs of reeds, each a different color, and made the first male and female human beings.

He put the sun in the sky to travel by day, and the moon to travel by night. He created cattle, goats and dogs, all wild animals, insects, birds and fish. Finally, he created water to drink and fire. He brought rain, the arts, health, and fertility. He even took care of the dead: they reside in the sky and their eyes are the stars.

But the creator god was also responsible for depriving men of immortality. He sent a chameleon to earth, carrying the gift of eternal life to all men. However, the divine messenger dawdled on the way. Meanwhile, Unkulunkulu had second thoughts, and sent a lizard with the message that all life would end with death. The lizard reached mankind before the chameleon, who arrived after men had accepted their fate. In compensation, Unkulunkulu instituted marriage so that human beings would grow in number.

He also taught people about themselves and nature, gave names and uses to all things, organized society and defined the roles of its members. Women were to fetch water and firewood, grind the corn, cook, dig the earth, and plant and grow millet. Their fathers would exchange them for cattle. Men had to guard the cattle, cut trees, build houses, and make tools for women to cultivate the earth.

✻

FOUNDER OF THE WORLD

✻

TURTLE
North America (Iroquois)

The Iroquois of the Great Lakes region of North America describe how, in the beginning of time, there was water everywhere peopled by creatures such as the beaver, the duck, and the muskrat. The mother of humankind, Aataensic, fell slowly from the sky with the first people in her womb, and all the creatures strove desperately to bring up from the depths a piece of soil on which she could safely land. The muskrat was successful, retrieving a clod of earth which he placed on Turtle's back just in time.

Aataensic landed safely and was able to bring mankind into being, while Turtle went on to support the world as the soil grew to enormous proportions on his back. The world still rests on his shell: when he stirs, the seas rise in great waves, and when he becomes restless, there are terrifying earthquakes. To many native North Americans today, the continent of North and South America is known as Turtle Island.

✻

CREATORS

❄

IZANAGI AND IZANAMI
Japan

Izanagi and Izanami were male and female *kami*, or sacred powers, the direct descendants of Kunitokotachi, the supreme heavenly being of Japanese mythology. Together they stood on the bridge of heaven, and stirred the primeval waters of the universe with a jeweled spear; the drops that fell from it created the first piece of land. Although they were brother and sister, they married and, in time, Izanami gave birth to mountains and trees, valleys and oceans; finally, she and her brother–husband added the islands of Japan as a special feature of their creation.

When Kagutsuchi, the god of fire, was born, the pain of his birth was so great that Izanami died. Inconsolable, her husband made his way to Yomi, the dark land of the underworld, in an attempt to bring her back to the land of the living; but his wife had been transformed into a decaying corpse. He fled, horrified by her appearance, and Izanami, angry at his betrayal, ordered evil hags, warriors, and thunder gods to follow him.

Although Izanagi escaped his demonic pursuers, he and his wife both realized that their marriage was over. Standing on either side of a boulder with which Izanagi had barred the entrance to Yomi, he and Izanami, by now a demon, agreed to part. Izanami became a goddess of the underworld, but Izanagi continued the act of creation and made the principal deities of the physical world: Amaterasu, the sun goddess, appeared from his left eye, and Tsuki-yomi, the moon god, came from his right one. Susanowo, the storm god, was born from his nose.

❄

The "wedded rocks" in Ise Bay are close to the great shrine of Ise, one of Japan's foremost centers of pilgrimage. According to legend they sheltered the sacred powers Izanagi and Izanami, the brother and sister who married and created the world's natural features.

❄

ALMIGHTY CREATOR

OLORUN
Africa (Yoruba)

Olorun, whose name means "the owner," is the almighty creator god of the Yoruba people of Nigeria. Invisible but omnipresent, he created the universe, night and day, the seasons, and the destiny of every human being who lived on earth.

The greatest of all gods, he owned the sky. He commanded Orisha Nla, the sky god, to go down to earth to lay a good foundation, and gave him three things: a snail shell with some earth in it; a pigeon; and a five-toed hen. Orisha Nla shook out the earth from the snail shell, the pigeon scattered it, and the hen scratched and dug it.

Next, Olorun sent the chameleon to inspect the land, which was found to be dry. So he sent Orisha Nla to plant four trees, among them the precious oil-palm tree. Then he sent the rain, vital for the growth of plants.

Finally, when all was tidy and organized, he ordered Orisha Nla to make sixteen human beings out of clay, men and women, of whatever shape or color he fancied. But only Olorun could give them life.

He also created death—as a gift to his people who, originally unable to die, became old and feeble, and prayed to Olorun to deliver them from their everlasting lives.

Although Olorun is the supreme god who "sees inside as well as outside men's hearts," there are no temples or priests to serve him. He is invoked only in times of greatest danger or catastrophe.

SUPREME RULER

SHANG DI
China

Shang Di has been the most powerful god of the Chinese pantheon for three thousand years. As a supreme deity, he eclipsed the sun,

Early images of Shang Di are rare: the supreme god of the Chinese pantheon was an abstract presence, the ancestor of the Shang Dynasty which lasted from c.1500–1050 BC. This statuette dates from about the fourth century AD.

moon, and earth in his powers, and reigned over heaven in the way that a dynastic ruler exercises power on earth. Today, as god of the sky, he exercises control over natural forces—thunder, lightning, wind, and rain. Credited above all with creating the universe from chaos and acting as its unifying principle, he is remote from people, an abstract controlling intelligence with no physical presence, and images of him are therefore rare.

To the first Christian missionaries, arriving in China after 1600, Shang Di seemed close to their one supreme god.

ALSO KNOWN AS: Yu Huang Shang Ti

MASTER OF THE WORLD

ZEUS
Greece

Supreme among the deities of the Greek pantheon, Zeus ruled heaven and earth from his home on cloud-capped Mount Olympus. Awesome in his power, he controlled the rain and caused lightning to flash to earth, when he was angered, by hurling his thunderbolt—his most famous attribute. He possessed an aegis, a shield that could terrify his enemies and protect his friends, and determined the outcome of battles. The personification of justice, he upheld the authority of the law and supported kings and rulers on earth. He was the god of marriage, the father, and the savior; the protector of men and women who were in search of sanctuary; and the deity associated with hospitality and harmonious relationships within families and between cities and states. Zeus was the son of Rhea, a Titan—a primordial deity—and her brother Cronos, who had first castrated his father Uranus and then usurped his position as king of the gods. To protect himself from a

The supreme deity of the Greek pantheon, Zeus was portrayed with remarkable consistency in all the many images that were made of him. The sculpture ABOVE dates from the first century AD, while those LEFT and RIGHT were created in the fifth and sixth centuries BC. All show him bearded and with copious locks.

RIGHT This image of Zeus is on a coin and reflects how the great god was a part of, and an influence on, the everyday lives of his worshippers.

BELOW The abduction and rape of Europa by Zeus, in the shape of a white bull, is a recurring theme in art. This portrayal is by Henry Fuseli.

RIGHT This sixth-century BC statue of Zeus shows him in characteristic pose. It is probable that he originally held a thunderbolt in his right hand. It was his most famous attribute and when he was angered, he hurled it and caused lightning to flash down to earth.

BELOW The temple of Zeus at Olympia originally contained a great statue of the god. Made of gold and ivory, it was created by Phidias—the fifth-century BC sculptor who also executed the sculptures on the Parthenon—and was one of the seven wonders of the ancient world.

similar fate, Cronos devoured his children as they were born. Only Zeus escaped when his mother smuggled him to safety and gave her husband a stone, wrapped in infant's clothing, to swallow. When the young god grew to manhood he overthrew the Titans and dethroned his father, whom he hurled into the great abyss of Tartarus, the underworld's place of punishment.

Zeus' first wife was the Titan Metis, the goddess of intelligence. Fearing that she would bear him a son who would become the leader of the gods, he swallowed her while she was pregnant. Their daughter Athena, goddess of wisdom, sprang from his forehead fully armed. The god later married his sister Hera and, despite her jealousy, enjoyed numerous affairs with his fellow deities and with mortals. His divine conquests included the Titan Leto by whom he had two children: Apollo and Artemis, deities of the sun and wild beasts respectively.

To deceive Hera, the god often took on different forms to visit his earthly lovers. He transformed himself into a shower of gold for his trysts with Danae, the daughter of the king of Argos. Perseus, the hero who decapitated the snake-headed Gorgon, Medusa, and rescued Andromeda from the dragon, was the result of this liaison. On another occasion, Zeus became a swan to seduce Leda, the wife of the king of Sparta. Their four children, hatched from two eggs, were Castor and Polydeuces (better known by his Roman name Pollux), the heavenly twins, and Helen of Troy and Clytemnestra, the wife of Agamemnon, hero of the Trojan war. As a white bull he abducted Europa, the daughter of a king of Tyre, and then changed into an eagle to ravish her. One of their three sons was Minos, the king of Crete, who presided over the Minotaur and the labyrinth in which the monster, half man and half bull, lived.

The god had affairs with men as well as women. When he fell in love with Ganymede, the beautiful son of a legendary king of Troy, Zeus transformed himself into an eagle and carried the youth to Mount Olympus to become the cup-bearer to the gods.

The epitome of manly prowess and strength, Zeus was especially honored at the great athletic festival held at Olympia—the forerunner of the modern Olympic Games, which even today provide a link to the supreme god.

This mosaic from Tunisia shows Zeus in the form of an eagle clasping Ganymede in his claws. He carried the beautiful youth to Mount Olympus, the home of the gods, to become cup-bearer to him and his fellow deities.

THE HIGHEST

VISHNU
India

Vishnu, the preserver, is the supreme god of the Hindu pantheon. As a manifestation of the sun as it rises, reaches its zenith and sets, he crosses the heavens each day with three great strides; and he is also associated with the division of the universe into earth, atmosphere, and heaven.

The embodiment of goodness, mercy, and morality, he is the enemy of Yama, the god of death, and the keeper of order. The great god is all-pervasive and has appeared on earth in nine avatars or incarnations, whenever some great evil has threatened human beings. His animal forms included Kurma, the tortoise, who carried on his

OPPOSITE TOP *In his incarnation as a fish, Vishnu warned Manu, the first human being, of the coming of a great flood and told him to build a boat; he later towed the vessel to safety.*

OPPOSITE BOTTOM *Vishnu rests on Ananta, the many-headed serpent of eternity. Lakshmi, his faithful wife, is at his feet and lotus flowers, symbols of both deities, bloom above and below them.*

LEFT *In his incarnation as Varaha, the boar, Vishnu rescued the earth when demons plunged it into the ocean: it took on the shape of a beautiful girl and Varaha raised it with his tusks.*

BELOW *This shows Vishnu resting on Ananta between the destruction of the world and the creation of the universe. It also shows him (top left) riding his mount Garuda, the sun bird.*

Demons and gods twine a serpent around Mount Mandara and make a paddle with which to churn the ocean. Vishnu sits on the mountain's peak and plans the cosmic order of the universe.

back the mountain, Mount Mandara, that the gods used as a paddle when they churned the ocean milk to create the sun and moon and other delights of the universe; and Varaha, the boar, who retrieved the earth when it plunged into the ocean. He was also Narashima, half man and half lion, who killed the demon Hiranyakashipu.

As a man, he was Rama, the hero of the epic *Ramayana*; and Krishna, the god who saved the world from the evil King Kansa who had usurped his birthplace. Vishnu's tenth incarnation is still to come: Kalki, a Messiah figure who will ride a white horse and whose appearance will herald the end of the world.

Vishnu was the creator of the wise god Brahma, who grew out of his navel, and of Shiva, the god of destruction, who was born from his forehead. As Vishnu-Narayana, he brought the universe into being through his own energy, by sucking his toe while drifting over the primeval waters on a banana leaf.

The great god is generally depicted as young and handsome. He is dark blue and has four hands; his symbols include the conch shell, a discus, and the lotus—he and his consort Lakshmi, the goddess of beauty and abundance and patron of wives, are often shown standing or sitting on this flower. His mount is Garuda, a sun bird whose father was Kasyapa, one of the primeval gods.

ALSO KNOWN AS: Visnu

LORD OF THE WORLD

✸

VIRACOCHA
South America (Inca)

The supreme creator god of the Incas of Peru, Viracocha was also a storm god and a sun god. He is usually represented as an old man with a beard, wearing the sun as a crown; he carries thunderbolts in his hands and weeps tears of rain.

But Viracocha was not an entirely beneficent god. Human sacrifices were required to appease him, and on special occasions, such as the coronation of an emperor at Cuzco, the Inca capital, children were taken to sacred places on frozen Andean mountain peaks and sacrificed to the god.

According to early legends, Viracocha fashioned the earth, sky, and stars with the help of his two sons. He first made mankind as a race of giants who lived in a dark world with no sun; but, displeased with his creations, he then engulfed the world in a great flood. The moon and sun emerged, with the moon brighter than the sun; but the sun dimmed the moon by throwing ashes at it. Meanwhile, the giants were replaced by smaller, better people, and the god wandered among them, dressed as a beggar, working miracles and teaching them the rudiments of culture. The living waters of Lake Titicaca were his tears, shed for the sufferings of his people.

Later Inca creation legends identified five ages. The first was the time of Viracocha, when the world was ruled by the gods and there was no death; the second was the age of the giants, worshippers of Viracocha; and the third was the age of the first primitive men. In the fourth age warriors ruled, followed by the fifth, the age of the Incas. This came to an end with the coming of the Spanish conquistadors in 1531. Viracocha himself then departed from Peru, and went out into the Pacific Ocean and over the horizon, walking on the water as if it were dry land, promising to return one day. Although the Inca elevated Inti, the sun god, in his place, they did not forget their debt to Viracocha.

✸

A creator, storm, and sun god, Viracocha shed tears for the sufferings of his people. This bearded, seated man wearing a headdress and earplugs is thought to represent him.

RULER OF THE WORLD

✸

SILA

North America (Inuit)

To the Inuit peoples of the Arctic regions of North America, Sila, a supremely powerful spirit, is the divine ruler of the world. From his domains far above the earth, he rules the souls of men and beasts and controls the sea and the elements—the wind, snow, and rain—around which Inuit existence revolves. Although he is generally benign, he must be propitiated with incantations and amulets, since offending him can result in extreme and dangerous weather conditions.

Despite his great powers, Sila remains the spirit of the air, without embodiment.

✸

CHIEF OF THE GODS

✸

ODIN

Northern Europe

The supreme god of the Norse pantheon, Odin was known by many names. He was the "all-father," the god of battle and the dead, magic and poetry. He was the deity of ecstasy and inspired the berserkers, Viking warriors who worked themselves up into a frenzy before performing insane acts of courage and daring on the battlefield.

Odin was also a creator god. He was the great-grandson of Audumla, a primeval cow

Odin rides Sleipnir, his eight-legged horse, in this detail from an eighth-century Viking stone. He is accompanied by Valkyries.

✸

who created his grandfather by licking the icebound rocks of the north to reveal first a man's hair, then his head, and finally his entire body. Odin and his brothers Vili and Ve fought and killed the frost giant Ymir, then chopped his body up and used its parts to fashion the mountains, cliffs, sky, and clouds of the physical world; the giant's blood became its oceans. They made mankind from two pieces of driftwood.

The supreme god was renowned for his wisdom, a gift that he obtained by giving one of his eyes to Mimir, the wisest of the gods, in return for permission to drink from his well at the base of Yggdrasil, the cosmic tree that overhangs the universe. To learn the secret of the runes, he hung himself on the tree for nine days. And for the inspiration of poetry, he seduced a giantess whose father owned a magical mead that turned anyone who drank it into a poet.

But he was also famously untrustworthy; he could be cruel and, although he was married three times to deities—Frigg the goddess of

This shows Odin in his human guise as a one-eyed, gray-bearded old man. The ravens who bring him news of the world are perched on his shoulder.

fertility, Jord the earth goddess, and Rind who ruled over frozen soil—he was notorious for fathering children with mortal women.

Odin rode a mighty eight-legged stallion called Sleipnir, and kept two ravens who brought him news. He used a spear carved with runic symbols to influence the course of battles, and was served by the Valkyries, beautiful maidens whose task was to visit battlefields and select the heroes who had died in battle and who were to enjoy eternal life in Valhalla, the god's hall of the slain. Every morning these warriors fought each other on the plain beneath Valhalla, and were restored to life every evening.

Like many of his fellow deities, Odin enjoyed wandering the world in human shape, often as an old, one-eyed man with a gray beard, wearing a brimmed hat and carrying a staff. But his earthly visitations could be terrifying. According to a twelfth-century legend, the people of Peterborough, in Northamptonshire, England, saw the god and heard a great number of huntsmen hunting. They were huge, black, and hideous; their mounts were black horses and black he-goats, and they were accompanied by jet-black hounds with eyes like saucers.

On the day of Ragnarok, when the gods meet their doom at the hands of the frost giants, the supreme god will be overwhelmed and killed by the forces of evil in the shape of the wolf Fenrir—monstrous offspring of the mischief-making god Loki—who will break free from his bonds and take his revenge on the deities who attempted to keep him in chains for eternity.

ALSO KNOWN AS: Voden, Woden, Wotan, Wuotan

A deity of magic and ecstasy, Odin was tireless in his search for wisdom and knowledge. He sacrificed one of his eyes to the wise god Mimir and hanged himself on Yggdrasil, the cosmic tree, suffering there for nine days to learn the secret of the runes. This image of the hanging god, half natural and half manmade, is carved into a rock formation in Germany.

LORD OF ALL KYNOWLEDGE

✳

THE DAGDA
Celtic (Ireland)

Literally "the good god," in the practical sense of being good at everything, the Dagda was also the all-father, lord of great knowledge, fire, and the god of magic. He controlled the weather and the crops, and was the protector and benefactor of his people. Immensely strong and with an enormous appetite, he owned an inexhaustible bronze cauldron from which no man ever came away hungry, and a great staff, one end of which could kill nine men at a stroke; the other end restored them to life. He also possessed two swine—one was always roasting and the other always growing—and trees that were forever laden with fruit. His consorts included the Morrigan, the queen of demons.

The Dagda was the chief of the Tuatha Dé Danann, ancient Irish deities of light and goodness. After their defeat by the ancestors of the Gaels it fell to him, as father of all the gods, to give each of his children a *sidhe*, or mound of earth, where they could live safely underground. Only one child was ignored: Aonghus Og, the god of love and the Dagda's son by the river goddess Boann. Aonghus, a beautiful young man above whose head four birds representing his kisses always hovered, owned Bruigh na Boyne, the palace of the Boyne, and although the Dagda wanted this dwelling place for himself, his son had ensured through trickery that it would remain the palace of the god of love for eternity.

Once his last task as all-father had been completed, and as the Tuatha Dé Danann disappeared into their *sidhe*, the Dagda resigned as their leader. His role as supreme deity was over; and his children, the gods, were transformed from deities to fairies. His attributes were the club, cauldron, and harp.

ALSO KNOWN AS: The Daghdha

GOD OF THE GODS

✳

WAKAN TANKA
North America (Lakota)

Wakan Tanka—the ultimate mystery— represents the creator or great spirit which underlies all things to the Lakota of the North American Plains. He is the god of gods, and all the other deities flow from him: the superior gods—sun, sky, earth, and rock—and associate gods—moon, wind, falling star, and thunderbirds. So, too, do the kindred gods: the two-leggeds—humans and their relatives the bears—the buffalo, the four winds, and the whirlwind. The remaining components are the godlike elements that include the shades of the dead and spiritual power. All sixteen elements make up Wakan Tanka, but he is greater than their sum total.

In prayer, the Lakota address the superior gods as "father," but invoke Wakan Tanka as "grandfather," to signify his ultimate authority. Throwing the ball, the final ritual in the sequence of Lakota pipe rites, represents Wakan Tanka and the attainment of wisdom.

✳

GIVER OF LIFE
❋

QUETZALCOATL
Central America (Aztec)

Quetzalcoatl—the feathered serpent—was one of the major gods of the Aztec pantheon and one of the four offspring of the original primordial being, Ometicuhtli. Quetzalcoatl's siblings were Xipe Totec, the flayed god of the east; Huitzilopochtli, war god of the south; and the black Tezcatlipoca, god of the night and the north; Quetzalcoatl himself represented the west. Cosmic struggles between the brothers, each of whom wanted to be the supreme deity, led to five successive world ages that were known as the five suns. Quetzalcoatl presided over the second age, known as four winds, but was cast aside by Tezcatlipoca.

He ruled a paradise reserved for those who had renounced earthly pleasures and who lived only for the spirit. As a creator deity, he descended into the land of the dead and picked up bones. On his return to earth, he sprinkled them with his blood and created humans. Quetzalcoatl had earlier been a god of

ABOVE Gentle and compassionate, Quetzalcoatl was regarded by the Aztecs with reverence and awe; something of his benign power is manifested in this greenstone statue.

RIGHT This manuscript illustration portrays Quetzalcoatl in his role as god of the wind. The bird shown here, known as the quetzal, is renowned for the beauty of its brilliant green, white, and red plumage. It was worshipped as the god of the air and associated with Quetzalcoatl.

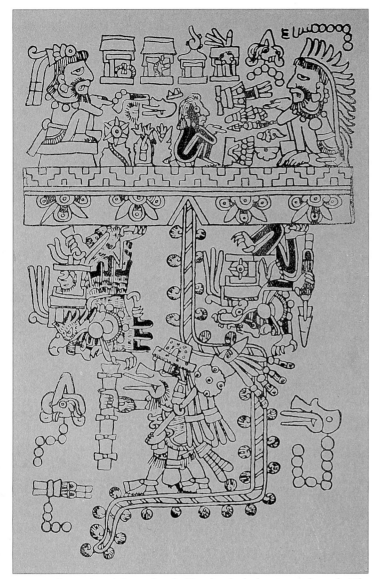

ABOVE Quetzalcoatl descends a ladder that links heaven with earth. The feathered serpent of Aztec mythology has been identified with a historical figure, a priest-king of the Toltecs who introduced the cultivation of maize in the tenth century, taught his people how to calculate the time and revealed to them the secrets of science and astrology.

BELOW This modern portrayal of Quetzalcoatl from a door in the Library of Congress, Washington DC, shows him in recognizably human form as a strong and vigorous ruler. The Aztecs believed that their god, exiled by Tezcatlipoca, would one day return and the Spanish conquistador Hernando Cortés took full advantage of this myth when he conquered and destroyed their state.

RIGHT This sculpture portrays Quetzalcoatl as the feathered serpent and reflects his early role as a deity of vegetation. Unlike his fellow gods he did not demand human sacrifice; rather, he was a lord of knowledge who taught wisdom to his followers and was a force for good in the Aztec pantheon.

BELOW Quetzalcoatl lifts the waters of the universal flood, a disaster that brought the fourth world age to an end, from the earth. Previous ages had been destroyed by jaguars, a hurricane, and fire. According to Aztec tradition the world is now in its fifth age and is awaiting a cataclysmic earthquake.

the Toltecs of Central America, whose traditions depict him as a rain deity, a synthesis of serpent and bird. To the Aztecs, he was god of the wind, the zodiac and the calendar, and a lord of knowledge—a gentle, compassionate deity who teaches wisdom to his followers and refuses to kill any living being.

Quetzalcoatl represented a force for good, but in the end Tezcatlipoca, his foe, finally triumphed over him. He used wine and necromancy to trick Quetzalcoatl into a liaison with his sister Quetzalpetlatl. Coming to his senses, Quetzalcoatl burned himself to death on a funeral pyre. Birds carried his heart into the night sky, where it became the planet Venus.

According to another legend, Tezcatlipoca tempted Quetzalcoatl into copulating with a demonic goddess. So he set fire to his palace made of silver and sea shells, buried his treasures and, wearing his green mask and feathered mantle, he left his city of Tula to sail eastwards on a raft of serpents, promising his people that he would return to them.

In taking over the cult of Quetzalcoatl, the Aztecs also inherited the Toltec myth that one day the god would reappear from the sea and claim his throne.

ABOVE This turquoise mask of Quetzalcoatl has teeth and eyes made from white shell. Birds, insects, and precious stones were sacrificed to him.

LEFT Quetzalcoatl's worshippers erected temples like this one at Teotihuacan, near Mexico City, in his honor. Another pyramid at Cholula, in central Mexico, was the new world's largest manmade structure when it was built.

MASTER OF ROME

✸

JUPITER
Rome

Jupiter, known also as Jove, was the all-powerful sky god of the Romans. In earliest times he was a manifestation of the sky, worshipped at the full moon and closely related to his Greek counterpart Zeus. As the best and greatest, he was worshipped with his consort Juno and daughter Minerva, goddess of wisdom, on the Capitoline hill in Rome. At first connected with agriculture, the weather, and light—the Ides, the days of the full moon, were sacred to him as was the full light of the sun—he came to have a special role as protector of the Roman people and also their benefactor: the Roman writer and politician Cicero declared that "Jupiter does not make us just sober or wise but healthy and rich and prosperous as well."

But the great god was able to unleash the forces of nature, letting loose thunderbolts and making the lightning flash. He was also associated with stones upon which oaths were taken and, since perjury was an offense severe enough to deserve punishment with a thunderbolt, another of his roles was to uphold oaths and treaties.

He developed a more benign role as guardian of the Latin league; each year in late April a feast was held on the Alban hills, when the leaders of Rome and her near allies celebrated their association with the sacrifice of a white heifer and a libation of milk.

Jupiter developed increasingly bellicose tendencies as the Roman Empire expanded: invincible and triumphant, he helped the Roman legions to stand firm in the field, and ensured that his victorious army gained plentiful booty. Finally, he acquired authority over the conquered peoples in the outlying provinces of the empire, where he was equated with local deities. Shrines to him in his embodiment as the Syrian weather god Dolichenus were constructed by Roman legionaries as far afield as Britain.

Meanwhile, back at Rome, Jupiter presided over games in the Colosseum, a vital part of Roman life, on September 4–19, October 15, and November 4–17. Triumphs—grandiose and lavish victory processions to celebrate successful military campaigns—ended at his temple on the Capitoline hill, and magistrates paid homage to him with sacrifices. Murderers and traitors to the Roman people were hurled

✸

The all-powerful Jupiter, special protector of the Roman people, holds a scepter, symbol of regal authority, and a thunderbolt—an attribute he shared with Zeus, his Greek counterpart.

✸

from the nearby Tarpeian rock. On certain market days, his priest, the *flamen dialis*, sacrificed a ram to him. And on September 13, the anniversary of the dedication of his temple, senators and magistrates sat down there to a banquet. Statues of Jupiter with Juno and Minerva, dressed in fine clothes, were placed at the table to join in the feast.

The advent of the Roman emperors— worshipped in their own right—circumscribed the god's power. No longer the representation of Rome's power and greatness, he found a new role as a more disembodied divine guide for the world: a supreme mind and intelligence who, from afar, controlled the destinies of men and women.

IDENTIFIED WITH: Zeus

The forum was the hub of ancient Rome where for many centuries the fate of the city, Italy, and Europe was decided under the tutelage of Jupiter. The great god's power and influence declined after the first century BC when Augustus became the first Roman emperor.

CHAPTER TWO

SUN

POWER

TSOHANOAI
North America

The native peoples of North America attribute enormous powers to the sun. To some it is the creator of the world, to others the brother or sister of the moon. Many myths describe how it was stolen, plunging the earth into darkness. In a Tanaina story from the far north, brave Raven rescues it from captivity, bringing back light to the human race.

Tsohanoai the sun-bearer, powerful sun god of the Navajo and husband of Estsanatlehi, goddess of the seasons, carries the sun on his back, and at night hangs it up on the wall of his house. A notorious adulterer, the god's nocturnal liaisons have produced numerous unpleasant monsters.

Native North American deities include culture heroes and tricksters like Coyote, as well as personifications of natural phenomena. The gods are believed to have come down to earth at mesae like these in Monument Valley, Arizona.

Many Plains tribes held, and some still hold, a yearly sun dance that lasts three or four days. It is intended to draw on the sun's powers to build up the health and strength of the participants, but the culmination is often their collapse in an exhausted trance. Injuries like the tearing of flesh, inflicted during the sun dance, signify liberation from the bonds of ignorance.

ALSO KNOWN AS: Johoonnaaei

POWER

TONATIUH
Central America (Aztec)

In the ancient Central American myth of the five suns—the five world ages—Tonatiuh represented the fifth age. He ruled over Tonatiuhican, the Aztec heaven, a spiritual paradise reserved only for the most worthy, such as warriors who had died in battle and women who had died in childbirth. As god of the east and the sun, his power was constantly

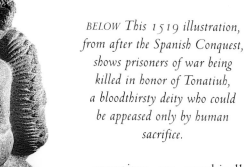

RIGHT *Tonatiuh inspired warriors in the heat of battle. A powerful deity, he represents the present, fifth, world age; here he wears an earthquake, the cataclysm that will bring it to an end, on his back.*

BELOW This 1519 illustration, from after the Spanish Conquest, shows prisoners of war being killed in honor of Tonatiuh, a bloodthirsty deity who could be appeased only by human sacrifice.

being burnt up through the colossal struggle of his daily birth, his passage through the heavens during the day, and his death at night. Fierce and warlike, he was also a deity of war who gave strength to soldiers in the heat and effort of battle.

Tonatiuh's spheres of influence meant that his power was always under threat, and the only way for mankind to maintain it was the exercise of high moral virtue—together with an endless cycle of human sacrifice. The god's appetites are graphically depicted in his images. His body, at the center of a large rayed solar disk, is painted red, and he wears a headdress of eagle feathers. His tongue is shaped like the sacrificial knife used by the Aztec priests to cut the hearts from their living victims— booty which is firmly grasped in Tonatiuh's giant claws. So notorious was the god's violence that the Aztecs named the most vicious of the Spanish conquistadors, Pedro de Alvarado, after him.

SUN

INTI

South America (Inca)

Inti, the Inca sun god, was a benevolent deity, as was his wife Mama Kilya, the moon goddess. To the Incas he was their ancestor, who had sent them to earth to propagate civilization. His cult was merged with that of the Inca kings who claimed him as their ancestor, and each year the mummified bodies of Pachacuti Yupanqui Inca, founder of the empire, and his queen, were taken on gilded biers in procession around Cuzco to the Coricancha, the temple of the sun. Here Inti's massive image, an enormous disk with rays fashioned in gold, was worshipped and revered in vast rooms full of precious objects, whose walls were covered in plates of gold—the sweat of the sun.

Inti's image at the Coricancha was surrounded by the mummified remains of dead emperors; the image of his wife, the moon—represented by a silver disk in a silver suite of rooms—was surrounded with their dead consorts. The god was served by the virgins of the sun. These were Inca girls taken from their families at the age of eight and enclosed in convents, from where they served the royal family as imperial concubines and maids, and kept alight the sacred flame for Inti Raymi, the main festival of the sun and crops, held over the June solstice—the shortest day.

Any family whose young daughter was chosen for sacrifice to the sun was greatly honored. After her ceremonial death the child would reappear in the form of an oracle, speaking through her brothers, who gained

The sun rises over Machu Picchu, high in the Andes. The city was sacred to the Incas, and the intihuatana, "the hitching post of the sun," is at its focal point.

rank and status. Inti also had a role in predicting cosmic events. His intihuatana, the hitching post of the sun at Machu Picchu—a pillar carved from the living rock that formed a ceremonial sundial—was the site of daily meetings of astrologers and wise men.

After the Spanish conquest, Christianity was a strong influence on Inti's cult, and a trinity of Intis developed: a father, son, and brother. The earth's diseases were seen as the manifestations of evil people who had lived before the coming of Inti the father. It was also said that the sun suffered from the same diseases as people, and infected the drinking water when ill. Rainbows were a sign that the sun was about to succumb to disease, and the signal for water to be collected and stored.

SUN

NZAMBI
Africa (Bacongo)

The sun god of the Bacongo people of Zaire, Nzambi is a fount of goodness, the ruler and sustainer of the universe, "the marvel of marvels." He protects and orders men, avenges injustice and shows kindness to all, even the most destitute. And he is the supreme judge after death.

According to one tradition, he created the first mortal couple and endowed it with intelligence. At first an androgynous being in the form of a palm tree, it eventually separated into two. It is often depicted carved out of wood with the head and breasts of a woman on one side, and a bearded head on the other.

It is said that once upon a time Nzambi fell out of the sky and lived on earth, but that he became afraid of men and retreated back to heaven by climbing a spider's thread.

The sun god, being inaccessible, has no cult.

ALSO KNOWN AS: Nzambe, Nyambe, Yambe, Zambi

SUN

APOLLO
Greece

Apollo was the brightest and best of the Greek deities, as skilled as he was beautiful. Although he was associated with the sun, he was also the patron of music and prophecy, archery and healing, and the protector of shepherds and their flocks.

He was the god of radiance, known as Phoebus or "bright" Apollo, and the epitome of young, virile manhood.

He and his twin sister Artemis, goddess of the moon, were the children of Zeus and a Titan called Leto. He was born on the island of Delos—the only land that would receive his mother as all other places feared the power of the god she would bear. At his birth he swore allegiance to his lyre and bow, and promised to reveal Zeus' will to mankind in oracles. At the age of four days he traveled to Delphi to kill a dragon that, reeking of blood, had attempted to molest Leto while she was pregnant. Apollo slew the serpent with an arrow from his bow. The site of his victory was at the exact center of the Greek world

Apollo was one of the twelve main gods in the Greek pantheon and he lived with them on Mount Olympus. Like them, he had his darker aspects: although he was a patron of medicine, his arrows could bring disease to human beings, and he could be merciless when he was enraged. When the mortal Niobe boasted that the fourteen children she had borne made her superior to his mother Leto, who had given birth to only two, Apollo slew her sons and the goddess Artemis, his sister, killed her daughters. And when the satyr Marsyas challenged him to a flute-playing contest, the god, infuriated at having his skill questioned, first won the competition and then had his challenger flayed alive.

He was also, like many of his fellow Olympians, renowned for his amorous exploits. But unlike them, he was often unlucky in love. One affair turned to tragedy when the mountain nymph Daphne changed into a laurel tree rather than yield to his embraces. Cassandra, daughter of Priam, the king of Troy, was a mortal who resisted his

and became one of his principal shrines. Here he made himself heard through the Delphic oracle, a priestess who, in a state of ecstasy brought on by the fumes of bay leaves, hemp, and other plants, replied to questions that ranged from the strictly personal to the political. Her utterances were often ambiguous and sometimes incoherent, but as the god's mouthpiece she was nevertheless consulted by visitors from all over the ancient world.

Apollo's temple at Delphi, seen here at the back of the amphitheater, was one of Greece's foremost shrines. Worshippers came from all over the ancient world to consult its priestess.

advances even though the god gave her the power of seeing into the future that she had demanded from him. Furious at her stubbornness, but unable to take back his gift, Apollo turned it into a curse: although Cassandra's prophecies always came true, they were never believed. An affair with Coronis, a Thessalian princess, ultimately had a more beneficent outcome—although she fell in love with a youth while pregnant by Apollo and was killed by Artemis at the sun god's command—their unborn child was saved and grew up to become Asclepius, the god of medicine.

The worship of Apollo continued well into the Christian era: it was the fourth century before the bright god admitted defeat. He told a messenger from the pagan Roman emperor Julian that his Delphic temple had fallen to the ground, and that he, "the shining one," no longer had a roof over his head.

SUN

SURYA
India

The son of the sky god Dyaus and Aditi, an ancient mother goddess, Surya holds a lotus flower in his hands as he rides across the heavens in a chariot drawn by as many as seven horses. His driver is Aruna, the dawn, whose appearance in the early morning marks the coming of the sun god.

Short, with a body the color of burnished copper, Surya's radiance was so overwhelming that his wife Sanjna took on the shape of a mare and fled to a forest to escape it—forcing

her husband to come to her as a stallion. Another consort of Surya was Lakshmi, goddess of beauty and abundance. Yama, the god of death, and the river goddess Yamuna are two of his children; others include Manu, an ancient deity of creation, and Revanta, a god of hunters. A daughter, also named Surya, is a sun goddess.

An image of Surya, god of the sun. His wife was overpowered by his radiance and, fleeing from her husband, took shelter in the shade of a forest. Her father later cut his son-in-law's substance by one-eighth to reduce his brightness.

SUN

✳

RE
Egypt

Re, an all-powerful and invincible sun god, began his life in the primeval waters. For a long time he resided in the heart of a lotus bud, and kept his eyes tightly shut so as not to lose his brightness. But one day he arose in all his shining glory, and became the god Re.

He first created human beings—some say from his tears—then ordered the annual inundation of the Nile which determined the seasons and brought fertility to the land that surrounded the river. He circumcised himself and, from the resulting blood, created Sia and Hu, personifications of the mind and authority; after which he reigned peacefully throughout his youth.

His main cult center was at Heliopolis, Greek for "sun city." In his aspect as Atum, the creator god, Re fathered air, Shu, and moisture, Tefnut, by his own means and gave birth to them by spitting them out of his mouth. The children of the brother and sister were the sky goddess Nut, and the earth god Geb. Incestuous unions continued among the deities until nine major gods, who were known

LEFT Every day Re sailed across the sky to the west. Every night he assumed a ram's head, symbol of life-giving properties, and sailed back to the east through the underworld.

ABOVE Pyramids were symbolic of sun worship. This small one shows Re as a falcon wearing the disk of the sun.

as the Great Ennead of Heliopolis, reigned over ancient Egypt.

Re's secret name, known to no one but himself—until the goddess Isis learnt it by trickery—had the power to give or take life when spoken aloud. Every morning he bathed before starting his daily task of sailing across the ocean of heaven from Manu, the sunrise hill, until he reached the western horizon. On the way, he visited the twelve provinces of his realm and spent one hour in each of them. Then he disappeared into the underworld, but in order to avoid depriving the world of light he created the moon.

Re's journey through the land of the dead was less peaceful. There the serpent of chaos, Apophis, reigned unchallenged. The demon lord of darkness loathed the sun god, and fiercely attacked him every night as he sailed across the waterways of the underworld to return to the east. But although Apophis had some near victories—once he swallowed the

ABOVE *Falcon-headed Re is shown here at his most powerful, wearing the uraeus— the golden cobra that symbolizes the power of instant death.*

RIGHT *As "lord of life in the underworld," ram-headed Re is taken by Isis and Nephthys to unite with their brother Osiris, lord of the dead.*

boat of the sun god during an eclipse, and spat it out again—he was always defeated.

King of the gods, Re was the god of the kings. They themselves claimed to be his descendants, and were regarded as his reincarnation: the pyramids that formed their tombs were dedicated to the sun. The pharaohs included Re in their name—a guarantee of their divine authority—and, following the example of his divine descendants, practiced incest within the royal family.

Re was represented as a man crowned with the solar disk, or with the head of a falcon surmounted with the *uraeus*, the sacred golden flame-spitting cobra that destroyed the god's enemies. Obelisks, whose points were first to receive his light at sunrise, were the symbols of his cult.

The sun god eventually became old and senile and, finding human beings to be too troublesome, left the earth to reside in the sky.

ALSO KNOWN AS: Ra, Phra
IDENTIFIED WITH: Amun, Atum

DIVINE KINGSHIP

HORUS
Egypt

Originally a great sky god, Horus appeared as a hawk or falcon, or with a falcon head, and ruled the air. His right eye was the sun, his left was the moon, but he became widely worshipped as the sun himself. His great sanctuary was at Edfu, where he was shown in the form of a hawk-winged sun.

A pendant in the shape of a falcon represents Horus. Made of gold and encrusted with lapis lazuli, turquoise and carnelian, it was found in Tutankhamen's tomb.

As the rising sun, he was identified with the king, who was said to be born on the eastern sky. Horus was the ancestor of all the pharaoh dynasties, and his name was always the first of the five names of the pharaohs.

"Horus of the horizon" was the name given to the Great Sphinx at Giza, the symbol of

A protective pendant shows the Eye of Horus, guarded by the royal cobra of Lower Egypt and the royal vulture of Upper Egypt.

Horus the falcon was lord of the sky. His name, "Har" in Egyptian, is generally interpreted as meaning "high above" or "far away."

divine kingship which looked eastward guarding the pyramid. The pharaoh Thotmes IV claimed that Horus had made him a king in exchange for clearing up the sand piled up around the sphinx.

Horus was the son of Isis the magician and Osiris, god of the underworld. Osiris had succeeded Geb as king of Egypt and had been assassinated by his brother Seth, who seized the throne. To avenge his father and claim his rightful inheritance, Horus fought a lifelong and murderous battle with his uncle.

Finally, after a war of eighty years, Horus triumphed over Seth and was awarded his right as the supreme ruler of Egypt. In the course of the conflict, Seth cut out his nephew's eyes—and was castrated in return—but Thoth restored the sun god's sight with divine saliva.

The eyes of Horus became a symbol of trustworthiness and protection. The *udjat*, or

Eye of Horus, was extended from its outer corner with falcon cheek marks below it, and was represented in many forms: as an amulet placed with a mummy, worn as a necklace, painted on the sides of coffins, and in Egyptian wall paintings.

IDENTIFIED WITH: Apollo

DIVINE PROGENITOR

AMATERASU
Japan

Amaterasu, the sun goddess, was one of the supreme deities of Japanese myth. She illuminated the world and was as beautiful as she was compassionate. Her father was Izanagi, a sacred power who had made the world with his sister–wife Izanami. She shared the universe with her brothers Susanowo, the storm god, and Tsuki-yomi, the moon god.

Amaterasu and Susanowo each wanted to be more powerful than the other and they agreed on the ultimate test: whichever of them could produce the most male deities would be the mightiest god in the Japanese pantheon. Amaterasu created three goddesses from her brother's sword and Susanowo riposted with five gods from her fertility beads. When the sun goddess claimed victory because her brother's deities came from her possessions, he went on the rampage and terrified Amaterasu and her attendant maidens.

Susanowo was tried by the gods and sent into exile, but the goddess nevertheless took refuge in the cave of heaven, leaving the world in darkness—and the other deities desperate for her to return to them.

To entice her, they hung a mirror outside the cave and, when a young goddess performed an erotic dance, laughed so loudly that Amaterasu was curious. She peered out of her refuge, saw the mirror and, intrigued by her own reflection, ventured out. As she did so, a nearby god pulled her away from the cave while another one barred its entrance with a magical cord. The goddess returned to heaven and once again poured the life-giving rays of the sun onto the earth.

Tsuki-yomi, like his brother the storm god, also displeased Amaterasu: he killed the food goddess Uke-mochi whom he believed had insulted him when, to entertain him, she used her mouth to furnish the mountains, land, and sea with food. The angry sun goddess reprimanded her brother for this deed, saying she would never see him again—the reason the sun and the moon live apart.

Amaterasu is also the divine ancestor of the Japanese imperial family. According to myth she dispossessed the earth god Ohonamoch, son of Susanowo, and made her grandson Ninigi the ruler of Japan. He married the goddess of Mount Fuji, and one of their great-grandchildren became Japan's first emperor.

ALSO KNOWN AS: Amaterasu-o-mi-kami

Enticed by her own reflection in a mirror, Amaterasu emerges from the cave to which she had fled in terror after an argument with her brother Susanowo.

CHAPTER THREE

※

EARTH, SEA, AND SKY

SEA

※

NJORD

Northern Europe

Njord, the handsome god of the sea, was one of the Vanir deities who were concerned mainly with bringing life and power into the world, rather than with justice and peace. But during a battle with the Aesir, a rival group of gods, he was taken hostage and ultimately came to represent a truce between the two races. His Vanir origins can still be seen in his roles as a beneficent god, protector of sailors and fishermen, who brings the life-giving food of the sea to human beings; and as an occasionally less beneficent one who controls the power of wind and storms.

He loved and married Skadi, a goddess of the far north and the daughter of a giant, who traveled on skis and hunted with a bow. But although they had two children—the twin fertility deities Frey and Freya—their union did not last: Njord could not live far from the sea while Skadi could not bear to leave her mountains.

OPPOSITE Uranus is shown at the top of this breastplate; Gaia, the earth, who was both his mother and his wife, is at the bottom.

RIGHT As the god of the sea, Njord had power over the wind and storms and would have been an important deity to seafarers like these Viking raiders, who depended on his goodwill for a successful outcome to their expeditions.

SEA

❋

POSEIDON
Greece

The brother of Zeus, the supreme god, and Hades, king of the underworld, Poseidon was one of the three great deities of ancient Greece. Awesome and powerful, he ruled over the oceans in his role as sea god; as the earth-shaker or earth-mover he was the creator of earthquakes. An old and bearded man, he traveled through the depths of the ocean in a chariot pulled by magnificent golden sea horses; and, easily enraged, used his mighty trident to stir the waters into a sudden storm if gods or mortals displeased him. In his beneficent moods he sent favorable winds and calm seas to speed sailors on their way. Poseidon was married to Amphitrite, by whom he had a merman son, Triton; but like his brother Zeus he had numerous love affairs, many of which reflect his association with horses, his sacred animal. One liaison was with the Medusa, the snake-haired Gorgon killed by the hero Perseus: the winged horse Pegasus, the child of her union with Poseidon, arose

Poseidon's influence spans the centuries but portrayals of the god may vary. The sculptor of the ancient Greek statue ABOVE *saw him as a man in the prime of life, strong and full of vigor, while the 1964 postage stamp* RIGHT *shows him as a young man. The figurehead* OPPOSITE *is modern but portrays the sea god in traditional style: he bears his trident in one hand and is driving the chariot drawn by sea-horses in which he traveled the oceans.*

This mosaic shows Poseidon surrounded by creatures of the sea. One of his children, by the goddess Amphitrite, was the merman Triton; a man above the waist and a fish below, he and other mermen were members of the god's court and accompanied him on his travels, blowing trumpets in the form of conch shells.

Poseidon, like his Roman counterpart Neptune, was a popular subject in art. Here Andrea Mantegna, the Renaissance painter, depicts a battle between the sea god and other mythological figures.

from her dead body. And he fathered another fabulous steed, Areon, from the goddess Demeter when she was in the form of a mare.

Poseidon's other lovers included Gaia, the earth, who gave birth to a giant, and Charybdis, a whirlpool in the Strait of Messina; but when he attempted to seduce Scylla, a beautiful nymph, his jealous wife transformed her into a sea monster with six heads and a girdle of barking dogs. She was positioned opposite Charybdis and together they formed one of the most dangerous hazards faced by Odysseus in his wanderings after the war against Troy, as well as by the Argonauts in their search for the golden fleece.

The Roman Neptune was an early god of water who was later identified with Poseidon. The two deities share the same attributes—a trident and a chariot drawn by splendid sea horses—but Neptune has an additional patronage. He is also the god of racetracks, a continuing link with the sacred horses of the great Greek god of the sea.

OCEAN

SUSANOWO
Japan

Susanowo was the son of Izanagi—a *kami* or sacred power who, with his consort and sister Izanami, created the world and its rulers—and the brother of Amaterasu the sun goddess and Tsuki-yomi the moon god. When the world was divided among the three children Susanowo, as the god of storms, was given particular responsibility for the ocean.

Impetuous and strong-headed, Susanowo angered the divinities of the Japanese pantheon by terrorizing his sister after losing a competition to prove which of them was the most powerful deity. His final act of aggression had been to skin a pony, and then hurl its body through the roof of a sacred hall in which Amaterasu and her maidens were weaving. The gods cut off his beard and banished him from heaven. Forced to live on earth, he conquered Korea and planted the mountains on Japan's Pacific coast with trees that grew from his hairs.

He married Kusa-nada-hime, the beautiful daughter of an elderly couple whose other seven daughters had been eaten by an eight-headed dragon. To save his intended bride from this fate, Susanowo changed her into a comb, and wore it in his hair while he made the monster drunk on *sake* and then hacked it to pieces. A magnificent sword that fell from its tail became part of the insignia of the Japanese imperial family.

ALSO KNOWN AS: Susano

SKY

NUT
Egypt

Nut is one of the most ancient deities in Egyptian mythology. As early as 3100 BC the high priests of Heliopolis (now Tell Hasan)—the most important religious center in the Egyptian world—determined the official version of cosmic creation. From Nothing arose Atum, the self-created supreme god who, "without the help of woman," produced Shu, the air, and Tefnut, moisture. They made Geb, the earth god, and his twin sister Nut, the sky goddess. The brother and sister became lovers, and from their union came the first of the most important deities of Egypt, including Osiris, the god of the underworld, and Isis, the magician goddess.

Nut's principal role as sky goddess was to receive and protect the dead. When their souls reached the heavenly vault formed by her body, they became the stars. Mother of the stars, Nut was also mother of the sun who passed through her body during the night and, from her nightly embrace with Geb, was born again in the morning.

The Egyptians regarded the coffin as a symbol of heaven—and therefore of Nut herself—and funerary pictures show the souls of the dead clasped against her star-studded bosom and enfolded in her wings. Her attributes were the sycamore, a papyrus scepter, and an *ankh*, symbol of eternal life. The hieroglyph of her name was a round vase, meaning heaven.

ALSO KNOWN AS: Nuit, Neuth

SKY

URANUS
Greece

The Greek god of the sky was first the son and then the husband of Gaia, the earth, the daughter of chaos, who bore him to give shelter to herself and future deities.

Their incestuous union produced twelve Titans—six sons and six daughters—three one-eyed giants called "bright," "lightning," and "thunder," and finally three ogres, each with a hundred hands. Uranus was so appalled by his offspring that he kept them pressed inside Gaia. In extreme discomfort she turned to Cronos, the youngest of her Titan sons, and pleaded with him to castrate his father; this he did, with an adamantine sickle, made by Gaia, when Uranus came to her that night. The drops of blood that fell from the sky god's wound were transformed into deities, nymphs, and giants; and his genitals, flung into the sea by his son, created a white foam which gave birth to Aphrodite, the goddess of love and desire.

The sky, emasculated, was separated from the earth; and Cronos became the king of the gods. He, in his turn, was deposed by Zeus, his son, the supreme god of the Greek pantheon, who flung him into the abyss of Tartarus in the depths of the underworld.

ALSO KNOWN AS: Ouranos

MOON

✷

IGALUK
North America (Inuit)

Igaluk is the moon spirit of the Inuit of the Arctic regions of North America, a powerful and skillful hunter who lives in the land of the sky. In Alaska, all creatures that are hunted for food and fur fall under his power—a role of immense significance because these animals are crucial to the survival of the Inuit peoples and are believed to have souls. The hunted animal gives itself up to the hunter, who must then ensure, by means of a short ceremony, that its soul is returned to its spiritual domain, ready, with Igaluk's help, to take on an earthly form once more.

Igaluk also has other roles as a guardian of morals and as a bringer of children: in both he must be propitiated with the help of a shaman—a healer or medicine person.

ALSO KNOWN AS: Tarqeq

✷

MOON

✷

SELENE
Greece

The Greek goddess of the moon, Selene was the daughter of two Titans: Hyperion, the god of primordial light, and his sister Thea. Her siblings were Helios, the sun god, and Eos, the goddess of dawn. The guardian deity of sorcerers and magicians, she

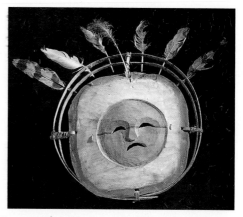

Inuit mask representing Igaluk, spirit of the moon. The board around the face is the air, the hoops encircling it are the levels of the cosmos, and the feathers symbolize the stars. It was probably worn by a shaman during propitiating ceremonies.

This vase painting depicts Selene as the waning moon, astride one of the horses that draws her chariot. The goddess and her mount are disappearing into the darkness of a moonless night sky.

drove a chariot drawn by two horses or mules across the sky, and was a powerful influence in the making of love charms.

The goddess herself fell in love with a handsome young shepherd called Endymion, while he was sleeping on Mount Latmos. So that she could enjoy his beauty forever, Selene caused him to sleep for all eternity.

———————— ✳ ————————

EARTH
✳

COATLICUE
Central America (Aztec)

The cult of Coatlicue—the serpent-skirted goddess—was centered on the Aztec capital Tenochtitlan, the site of which lies under modern Mexico City. The creator goddess of the earth and mankind, she fed on human corpses, and was also responsible for fire and for the springtime; curiously, she added to this a responsibility for florists.

Coatlicue was the wife of the war god Mixcoatl, to whom she bore four hundred sons, the stars, and a daughter, Coyolxauhqui, the moon. While sweeping her home, the serpent-mountain at Tula, the goddess was impregnated by a ball of feathers, and her children decapitated her to punish her apparent dishonor. But Huitzilopochtli, the sun god, sprang fully armed from her body and slew his brothers and sister, thus turning day into night. This epic battle was regularly commemorated at the great temple at Tenochtitlan, where women were thrown down the temple steps to their deaths in memory of the slaying of the goddess.

A vast statue of Coatlicue, originally at the great temple, bears testimony to her hideous and awesome appearance. She stands on huge taloned feet and wears a skirt of rattlesnakes. Her grotesque, pendulous breasts are partly hidden by a grisly necklace of severed human hearts and hands, from which hangs a skull. Thirteen leather cords decorated with snails hang on her back, symbolizing the mythical

Coatlicue, the fearsome earth goddess of the Aztecs, wore a skirt of writhing serpents and lived on a diet of human corpses. Her 400 sons became the stars of the southern hemisphere.

heaven. In place of a head and hands, writhing snakes emerge from her severed throat and wrists, and two enormous serpents of blood form her face. This mutilated and grotesque mother of the gods could be propitiated in only one way—with human sacrifice.

———————— ✸ ————————

EARTH
✸
GEB
Egypt

The Egyptian earth god Geb is unusual in that he is male: most cultures regard the earth as a divine mother. He is depicted as a man stretched out on his back, with a green body that represents vegetation germinating. His phallus is in perpetual erection in an attempt to reach his twin sister Nut, the sky goddess who forms the celestial arch above him. The incestuous twins had been separated on the orders of their grandfather, Re-Atum, who disapproved of their union because he had not been consulted. Their passion nonetheless bore fruit in the form of the

greatest divinities of Egypt, Osiris, god of the underworld and his sister and wife Isis, the magician goddess.

The ruler of the world, Geb was greatly feared for his laughter which provoked devastating earthquakes. Yet he was also regarded as a benign fertility god, who provided all living creatures with nourishment.

———————— ✸ ————————

HEAVEN
✸
AMIDA
Japan

The "Buddha of infinite light," Amida is a bodhisattva, one of the divine beings who, although worthy of nirvana and therefore absorption into Brahma, remains with human beings to help them to salvation. The god of heaven, he brought solace to all mankind. Amida had forty-eight wishes, one of which was that the dead should come to the land of Jodo over which he would preside, and be allowed to live here until they are finally released from the cycle of reincarnation.

———————— ✸ ————————

Geb the earth god and his twin sister Nut the sky goddess are depicted acting out one of several Egyptian creation myths. Geb's body is green to indicate vegetation, while his limbs represent mountains and valleys.

———————— ✸ ————————

Anyone who invokes the god's name with a pure heart is reborn in this paradise. There, trees bear jewels instead of fruit, and their branches, on which perch brilliant birds, are hung with bells; a lotus pond is full to the brim with ambrosia, and angels scatter petals over the god, who is seated on a lotus, and over his attendants.

In art Amida is surrounded by a huge halo and has two attendants: Kwannon, the goddess of mercy and Seishi, the lord of might. A gleaming spot on his forehead is symbolic of his wisdom.

IDENTIFIED WITH: Amitabha

LEFT *Amida is seated on a lotus flower. The halo that surrounds his head and the gleaming spot on his forehead are his two most familiar attributes.*

RIGHT *Amida raises his hand in a gesture of blessing. In the background he is shown with his attendants Kwannon and Seishi.*

THUNDER

THOR
Northern Europe

Thor was vigorous and hot-tempered, a mighty figure who was in many ways more like one of his arch-enemies, the frost giants who constantly plotted against him and his fellow deities, than a god. Red-headed and red-bearded, he had a voracious appetite for both food and drink and was the strongest of all the gods. He had three magic weapons: a girdle that could double his already enormous strength; a hammer, called Mjölnir, which created

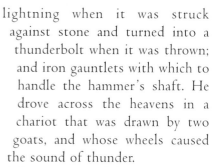

lightning when it was struck against stone and turned into a thunderbolt when it was thrown; and iron gauntlets with which to handle the hammer's shaft. He drove across the heavens in a chariot that was drawn by two goats, and whose wheels caused the sound of thunder.

The epitome of dynamic Nordic manhood, Thor was worshipped as a beneficent deity concerned with the administration of justice, one who protected both gods and men from evil and destruction,

ABOVE *This amber figurine, probably a chessman, encapsulates the benign vigor of the god of thunder.*

One of Thor's most famous exploits was his sea battle with, and victory over, the Midgard serpent. The plaque LEFT *shows him fishing for it, with the help of the giant Hymir. In the illustration* OPPOSITE *he is wielding his hammer against the monster.*

RIGHT *Thor's hammer could create thunder and lightning; but it was also a symbol of the god's beneficence and was used to bless infants and brides.*

The bronze statuette of the god ABOVE RIGHT shows him holding an ax, a symbol of fertility and another of his attributes. The swastika, shown clearly in the image ABOVE, may have been derived from this symbol.

who brought fertility to the fields and happiness in marriage, and to whom sacrifices were offered when plague or famine threatened.

He was constantly engaged in action and adventure, and one of his most famous exploits was his battle with the Midgard serpent, the fearsome monster that encircles the world awaiting its end.

Thor went out to sea with the giant Hymir who was at first alarmed at the speed with which the boat traveled when the god took the oars; and then terrified when the great serpent took the bait—an ox-head—that was thrown out to it and became hooked on the line. Thor used all his strength to haul it in, pushing his feet through the boat and standing on the bottom of the sea. As the serpent's head appeared, and god and monster stared into each other's eyes, the terrified Hymir cut the line and the serpent was able to disappear in the depths of the ocean.

The god then knocked the giant into the sea and waded back to the shore.

Thor's next, and final, encounter with the Midgard serpent will be at Ragnarok, the day of doom when the forces of evil overcome the gods and their allies.

As the Fenrir wolf breaks the fetters that bind it, and then swallows the sun and bites the moon, and as the serpent causes clouds of poison to overwhelm both earth and sky, the mighty god Thor will fight and kill his monstrous enemy—and die.

THUNDER

THUNDERBIRDS
North America

Thunderbirds, the terrifying and powerful manifestations of thunder in spirit form, are widely found in the myths of the native North Americans. Almost unimaginably vast, they flash lightning from their eyes or beaks and make thunderclaps when they move their massive wings.

They engage in continual battles with horned serpents and with other malevolent monsters of the deep—earthquakes, floods, and terrifying thunderstorms are the earthly result of these clashes—and in the Yukon, in northwest Canada, they snatch whales, on which they prey, from the seas.

Among the Lakota, Thunderbirds sometimes possess certain human beings through dreams, and play malicious tricks on them, for instance making them behave contrarily—some wear warm winter clothes during the hot summers of the Great Plains. But the spirits can also confer benefits, such as granting healing powers on those they possess, or sending rain to sustain the growth of food and vegetation.

ABOVE Thunderbird is depicted above four horses on the back of a beaded Sioux vest. Ceremonial garments like this one were traditionally made by women.

LEFT Headdresses like this Thunderbird one were worn by human impersonators of native North American deities during ritual ceremonies.

CHAPTER FOUR

※

THE NATURAL WORLD

VEGETATION

※

ADONIS
Greece

Adonis, god of vegetation, was a beautiful youth from Cyprus, born of incest between Princess Myrrha and her own father, the king of Cyprus, a union masterminded by Aphrodite who had become jealous of the girl's beauty. When the king realized he had been tricked he tried to kill his daughter. But the gods protected her and changed her into a myrrh tree, from which Adonis came forth.

Aphrodite, after first hiding him in a chest, adopted the boy who grew to become the epitome of manly beauty. Overwhelmed by his good looks, the goddess fell helplessly in love with him and accompanied him everywhere. One day, however, ignoring her warning, Adonis went hunting on his own and was mortally wounded by a wild boar. Aphrodite rushed to his side but was too late to save his life. Anemones, the Adonis flowers, are said to have sprung from his blood.

The goddess was devastated and asked her father for help. Zeus brought Adonis back to

ABOVE This eighteenth-century marble sculpture by Giuseppe Mazzuoli captures the moment when the vegetation god is attacked and wounded by a wild boar.

OPPOSITE Aphrodite tends her lover Adonis, who is bleeding to death. Eros assists her.

life, but on condition that he spend only part of his time on earth and the rest in the underworld.

The death and rebirth of the beautiful god were celebrated with the Adonia festival in Athens in midsummer.

Adonis gardens, pots of flowers and herbs that—like the god and the vegetation he represented—swiftly bloom, wither, and die were used in the festivities, which included funereal ceremonies and orgiastic rites in which priests wearing feminine clothes slashed themselves with knives.

IDENTIFIED WITH: Attis

Persephone holds a pomegranate, one of her symbols, in her right hand. Because she had eaten a seed from the fruit she was forced to spend part of the year in the underworld.

VEGETATION

PERSEPHONE
Greece

Persephone, the goddess of vegetation and the queen of the underworld, was the daughter of Zeus, supreme god of the Greek pantheon. As a young child, playing in a meadow, she caught sight of a remarkable narcissus with a hundred flowers, planted by Gaia the earth-mother goddess as an offering to Hades. As she bent to pick it, Hades, god of the underworld, rose through a chasm and carried her away to his dark realm.

The earth paid a terrible price for this abduction. Springs ran dry, vegetation dried up and animals stopped breeding. And Demeter, mother of Persephone, wandered the barren world with two flaming torches mourning her daughter.

In the end, Zeus ruled that his brother Hades could not keep the girl as his bride without her consent. However, she had eaten a pomegranate seed on Hades' orders, and because of this the god was permitted to keep her in the underworld for part of the year, in the months following the harvest, while she spent the fertile months with her mother on Mount Olympus.

This myth was re-enacted each year at Eleusis, close to Athens, as part of the sacred mysteries, and gave Persephone a role, with her mother Demeter, as a goddess of vegetation who made the corn grow. She also had a darker side through her connections with death and the dead.

Her emblems were an ear of corn and a pomegranate seed. Proserpina was her Roman counterpart.

THE SEASONS

✴

ESTSANATLEHI
North America (Navajo)

To the Navajo people of the North American southwest, the changing seasons of the year are an expression of their life-force deity: Estsanatlehi or Changing Woman.

She endlessly repeats the human cycle of life from youth to old age, just as the seasons follow each other, and at the same time changes both her names and her clothes; she is also called Jet Woman, Whiteshell Woman, or Turquoise Woman.

Born of human parents, First Man and First Woman, Changing Woman created the Navajo people, perhaps from balls of white and yellow maize, or perhaps by rubbing the skin from her body into balls. She then went into the west where she became goddess of the sunset land, and sent all good things to the Navajo—the snow, the spring, plants, and maize—and won their love and devotion. But her parents, First Man and First Woman, who lived in the east, were her bitter enemies and it is they who were responsible for evils: wars, plagues, and white men.

✴

RAIN

✴

LEZA
Africa

A chief god in Zimbabwe, a high god in Zambia, a sky god in Angola, Leza was above all a rain bringer. But despite his beneficence, men were afraid of him. One legend

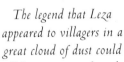

The legend that Leza appeared to villagers in a great cloud of dust could well have originated in this Zaire village on its border with Zambia. Storms and hurricanes are frequent and frightening occurrences in that region.

tells how he summoned the honey bird to heaven, and gave him three calabashes, or gourds, to take to the first men on earth. Two of them contained seeds, but the third was not to be opened until Leza himself came down to give instructions about its contents. Unable to control his curiosity, the honey bird opened the calabash while flying down to earth, and in so doing irretrievably unleashed on the world wild beasts of prey, dangerous snakes, disease, and death.

Leza controlled lightning and thunder as well as rain, and the appearance of thick clouds meant that his anger was about to explode. Lightning meant he had exposed himself, and thunder, that he had belched. One day, he summoned all the wild animals on earth, and provided them with tails to chase away the flies. The rabbit and the shrew mouse failed to turn up on time—and there were no tails left for them.

There is a tradition that Leza once lived with men under a great tree and was visited by devotees who brought him goats and sheep for food. One day, the god told a worshipper who had just brought him four goats to go back to his village and announce the coming of Leza. The villagers gathered together and saw a great cloud of dust approaching, followed by a hurricane and torrential rain. Leza arrived and said, "From now on you must honor my house. As for me, you will never see me again."

And he disappeared for ever.

But when people see shooting stars, they say that Leza is taking a look at the earth to see how his children are faring.

SOMETIMES IDENTIFIED WITH: Nzambi

RAIN

TLALOC
Central America (Aztec)

A pre-Aztec rain god adopted by the Aztecs, and with a close affinity to the Mayan rain god Chac, Tlaloc was one of the most powerful gods in the Aztec pantheon. His shrine, painted white and blue, shared the summit of the great temple at Tenochtitlan with that of the mighty Huitzilopochtli. As the bringer of rain, which could be beneficent or destructive, his continued benevolence was essential to his worshippers, and at the end of the dry season many small children were ritually sacrificed on mountaintop altars to ensure that a season of plenty would follow. Their weeping was considered an auspicious omen as their tears symbolized plentiful rain.

Tlaloc created and ruled a pleasant heaven, Tlalocan, for those who had died at his hands through drowning or being struck by lightning. In this earthly paradise, a land of water and mist located partly in the cloud-capped mountains and partly in lakes and streams, his chosen ones passed their time in earthly enjoyment, with an abundance of food, flowers, and beautiful things. Here, Tlaloc resided in caves and kept four great jars. From the one in the east he dispensed gentle rain to fertilize crops—his name means "he who makes things sprout." But from the others he poured out drought, disease, and frost, all of which were harmful to mankind.

Tlaloc could also control lightning and mountain springs and conceal himself behind a storm cloud. Representations of him show a black body with a painted face, protuberant

Tlaloc brings water to make the corn grow. This illustration is a replica of a fresco in one of the pyramids at Teotihuacan, Mexico's ancient religious center.

This relief from the side of an Aztec temple shows Tlaloc with the god of the morning star. Children were sacrificed to the god of rain on mountaintop altars.

eyes, and four large jaguar teeth—perhaps because thunder could be equated with the growls of this large cat. The staff he carries in his hands is a symbol of lightning; it may be entwined with teeth or snakes.

IDENTIFIED WITH: Chac

RAIN

CHAC
Central America (Maya)

Chac, the Mayan god of rain, has been worshipped in various forms continually for longer than any other deity in Central America, where the great variations in the climate, from dry and arid to tropical rain forest, give him a special importance. Vast in size, he was regarded by the Maya as a friend of mankind who had taught people agricultural skills, and as being responsible not just for bringing rain, but for wind, lightning, bread, and the fertility of crops on small farms. He is depicted as a red man with a long pendulous nose, catfish whiskers, and reptilian scales, and often wields lightning or a torch.

In later myths there were four Chacs, each a different color, who were important but lesser gods of thunder and lightning. They represented the four points of the compass and were known as the urinators, because rain fell from between their legs. The hearts of wild animals were sacrificed to them during the spring festival.

Under Christian influence, the Chacs have become small bearded figures who live in the

ABOVE One of the earliest Central American deities, Chac is also one of the most long-lived. This sculpture dates from 1300 to 1000 BC and portrays the god of rain in human form.

LEFT Masks representing Chac line the stairway of the pyramid of the magician at Uxmal, a Mayan center on the Yucatan peninsula in Mexico that flourished between the seventh and ninth centuries.

sky and are obedient to the will of "Jesucristo." They ride through the air on horses carrying gourds of water, from which they produce heavy rain, or lighter showers. Inveterate smokers, they throw away their cigarette ends as they ride; these are seen on the earth below as shooting stars.

IDENTIFIED WITH: Tlaloc

RAIN

✳

TONINILI
North America (Navajo)

Rain is brought to the Navajo of North America by Water Sprinkler, Toninili, the water-carrier of the gods. The companion of Black God, the god of fire with whom he played an important part in the creation of the world, Toninili holds sway over all the rain clouds in the sky.

But like the rain, Toninili can play tricks on mankind. During the night way and other ceremonies in which he and his fellow Yei—the lesser gods—take part, people impersonate him and his companions, and take on their characteristics.

During the ceremonies, the human counterpart of Toninili dances purposely out of step and trips up the other Yei. And frequently, engrossed in his own dancing, he stays long after the ceremony has come to an end.

VOLCANIC FIRE

PELE
Oceania (Hawaii)

Pele, Hawaiian goddess of volcanic fire, embodied the power of destruction. With her jealous nature and violent temper, she exhausted her family who eventually drove her out of her home in Tahiti. The goddess stole her brother's canoe and, after a long voyage, arrived in the northern islands, preceded by red clouds and flashes of lightning. She searched for a place to live, but every time she started to dig the ground the sea poured in and she was forced away. Eventually she reached Hawaii, where she dug herself safely into the solid rock of the great volcano, Mount Kilauea.

Although she settled there, her temper did not improve. She was also unpredictable, and when she was angry she turned all living beings into stone by overwhelming them with a flow of lava.

Pele was also a goddess of hula magic and sorcery, and constantly maltreated people. One night, she took the form of a beautiful woman and went to a hula dance, where she seduced Lohiau, a handsome young chief. After three days of love she left, promising to send for him. But when she finally returned, accompanied by her three sisters who had come to live with her, Lohiau had died of longing. She restored him to life with her sisters' help; but they admired the handsome young man too openly for her liking. Full of jealousy, she set fire to all of them.

Pele became important in Hawaii, where volcanic eruptions are frequent, and many altars were erected to her beside lava streams.

This wooden statuette of Pele has shell eyes and real hair. Legends about the goddess emphasize her jealousy and unpredictability.

WIND

AMUN
Egypt

Originally the local deity of Thebes, Amun was god of the wind and ruler of the air. His name means "the hidden one" or "invisible," and his image was never represented in the hieroglyphs. A powerful god, he created the sky and the earth with his thought.

When the city of Thebes became the capital of the Egyptian empire, Amun's status rose. He became god of Egypt, king of the gods, patron of the pharaohs, and was soon associated with the great sun god Re as Amun-Re.

All-powerful, he chose and deposed kings as he wished. In 1354 BC, a young pharaoh acceded to the throne and declared the cult of Amun to be the official religion of the empire. He took the name of Tutankhamen.

The god's fame spread though Egypt and beyond. Even Alexander the Great recognized his power and consulted his oracle. Immensely rich, Amun owned three-quarters of the wealth of all the other deities combined; and over eighty thousand slaves

ABOVE Amun wears the crown of the sky god surmounted by two high plumes representing the Two Lands, Lower and Upper Egypt. He holds before him the young king Tutankhamen who reinstated the cult of Amun.

RIGHT Shown here is one of the avenues leading to Amun's temple in the Karnak sanctuary. It is lined with ram-headed lions, each one protecting a statue of the pharaoh between its front paws. The ram was one of the god's sacred creatures.

*At modern Karnak, on the eastern bank of the Nile, stands the Great Temple of
Amun. Originally built in the second millennium BC, it included great colonnades,
part of which can be seen here. All the columns were entirely decorated with scenes of
worship and religious festivities. Carvings showing pharaohs in the presence of the god
emphasized the link between Amun and royal power.*

LEFT *This jeweled pendant from the sixteenth century BC represents a religious ceremony. The king in the center, described in the hieroglyphs on either side of him as "the favorite of the gods," is sailing in a boat, presumably on the Nile. The god Amun stands on the king's left, and the falcon-headed god Re on his right. Together, they are pouring the purifying water over the king's head.*

RIGHT *The great temple built by Rameses II in c.1250 BC, at Abu Simbel in Nubia, was dedicated to Amun, Re, and Rameses himself. Shown here are the four colossi representing the pharaoh, guarding its entrance. Carved out of the mountain and facing the Nile, they are 60 feet (20m) high. Many temples were built in honor of Amun in Nubia, the rich province from which the pharaohs imported gold and precious woods.*

were assigned by the pharaoh Rameses II to service his magnificent sanctuaries at Karnak and Luxor; only about twelve thousand were given to the great god Re at Heliopolis.

Amun was the only Egyptian god to have been served by priestesses. Considered to be his earthly wives, they remained celibate and the succession was assured by adoption. His priests were ruled by the high priestess, who attained royal status. They owned one hundred and sixty towns in Egypt and nine in the Middle East. A wonderful festival was held in the tenth month of every year, during which the god visited the "gods of the West," in the underworld. He sailed across the Nile from Karnak in a huge, sumptuous gilded boat called *Ouserhat*, made of Libyan wood and covered in precious stones. The pharaoh took part in the procession on land, which included chariots, musicians, acrobats and dancers, and stopped at all the royal temples.

Because Amun was as mysterious as the movement of the wind, he was naturally associated with the mystery of creation, and was believed to have made the air which gave life to human beings. He is depicted in the form of a man, often sitting on a throne. His body is the colour of lapis lazuli, an imported, expensive precious stone, signifying his great wealth and status. He wears the crown of a sky god, topped by two ostrich feathers that were divided vertically into two sections, for North and South Egypt, and into seven segments—a number believed to be magical.

Other depictions of the god Amun show him as a fertility deity with a hugely erect phallus, or in the shape of a ram— he was believed to be incarnated in a sacred ram kept in the sanctuary at Karnak. His sacred animals were the ram and the goose.

Among several other powers and attributes, Amun was believed to be a magician and healer. He preserved corpses, cured scorpion bites, offered protection from lions, snakes, and crocodiles, and ensured fair play for the poor.

ALSO KNOWN AS: Amon, Ammon, Amen
IDENTIFIED WITH: Re, Zeus, Jupiter

✳

Egyptian gods were clean-shaven, unlike their worshippers, and false beards, plaited and turning up at the tip, indicated their divine status. The god Amun also holds the ankh, symbol of life, in one hand, and the scepter of royal power in the other. His headdress, a kind of mortar board, was usually surmounted by two high ostrich feathers.

RIVERS

GANGA
India

Ganga is the guardian deity of the Ganges River, and was at different times the consort of three great gods of Hindu mythology: Vishnu, Agni, and Shiva. A river goddess, she emerged from one of Vishnu's toes and flowed into the heavens. It happened, however, that there was a terrible drought. Men and women were desperate for moisture, and it became obvious that the only way to return life-giving waters to the parched land was to bring the goddess—the personification of the Ganges—to earth. But the sacred river was so vast that her fall would have caused floods and devastation. To prevent this disaster, Shiva allowed her waters to flow through his matted locks until their force had been tamed, and then released the goddess to continue her descent.

Ganga has two or four arms, is white and is often portrayed riding a fish. She carries a water pot and a lotus.

This river goddess is carrying a water pot, one of the symbols of Ganga, goddess of the Ganges.

WOODS

PAN
Greece

The god of fields, woods, shepherds and flocks, Pan was a long-haired and shaggy deity with the body of a man but the legs, horns, and ears of a goat. He haunted the grottoes and lonely places, mountaintops and rock-strewn paths of his native Arcadia, where he made sheep and goats prolific and helped hunters to kill wild beasts.

His father was Hermes, the messenger of the gods, and his mother was probably Dryope, daughter of King Dryops: it is said that when Pan was born she fled in terror from her half-man, half-animal son, and that his father took him to Olympus where the gods were delighted with his appearance and his merry laughter.

The grown Pan was bearded, with a wrinkled face and prominent chin. Playful, energetic, he could also be ill-tempered, especially if he was disturbed while sleeping, and he delighted in appearing out of the hot blue haze of noon to terrorize men and animals—hence the word "panic." He embodied male sexuality and all his myths are concerned with his amorous affairs. The most famous describes his pursuit of Syrinx, one of Artemis' attendant nymphs, who escaped him only when her father, the river god Ladon, turned her into a

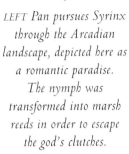

LEFT *Pan pursues Syrinx through the Arcadian landscape, depicted here as a romantic paradise. The nymph was transformed into marsh reeds in order to escape the god's clutches.*

RIGHT *This portrayal of Pan with one of the many nymphs who inhabited Arcadia depicts him as coarse featured and shaggy haired, with the legs and horns of a goat.*

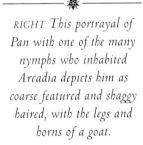

bed of marsh reeds. The sweet, sad sound of the wind blowing through the reeds so entranced the god that he fashioned two of them into one of the most ancient of musical instruments: the pan-pipes.

Pan was originally a purely Arcadian god, but shortly before the Athenians and the Persians met at the battle of Marathon, he told the Athenian ambassadors to Sparta that he would vanquish their enemy if they promised to worship him in Athens. The Persians were defeated and the Athenians later erected a sanctuary for him on the Acropolis.

There is a longstanding tradition that Pan died at the exact moment that Christ was crucified; that a seafarer near Italy heard a voice say, "Tell them that great Pan is dead," and that a sound of great weeping was heard at the news. To many early Christians this was the beginning of the end of paganism; and by the late Middle Ages the ancient god of the Greeks was identified with the devil.

Pan's Roman counterpart was Faunus. A temple was erected to him on the Tiber island.

❋

GREEN LAND

❋

BALDER
Northern Europe

Handsome, gentle, and gracious, Balder was the god of light and the most beloved of the Norse gods who lived in Asgard. His name means "bright" or "the shining one" and he lived with his wife Nanna and blind brother Hoder, the god of darkness, in a hall called Breidablik. He was a master of herbal medicine, and taught human beings how to use herbs for healing. Balder was the favorite child of his parents, Odin and Frigg, and when he had nightmares and dreams that threatened him with a terrible fate his mother asked everything in the world—animate and inanimate—to swear an oath that they would not harm her son. Only the mistletoe—puny, soft, and insignificant—was neglected.

For some time after all natural objects had given this promise, the gods and goddesses amused themselves by flinging rocks and darts at him, knowing that they could not harm him. But Loki, the wizard of lies, was jealous of his beauty and popularity, and eventually gave a dart of mistletoe to Hoder and aimed it for him at Balder. The god of light died and all of Asgard mourned.

Frigg, distraught at the loss of her son, suggested that it might yet be possible to rescue him from the underworld; and Odin sent their third son, Hermod the Bold, to plead with Hel, its queen, for Balder's release. For nine days and nights, Hermod rode through the dark valleys that surrounded the underworld. He crossed the bridge of the dead, and for three nights he stayed in the hall where Balder was sitting, and begged the queen to allow his brother to return to Asgard. She agreed, on condition that every object in the world should weep for him.

The gods sent messengers throughout the world to tell all created things how Balder could be saved and the sound of weeping was soon universal. Only Loki refused to shed even a tear; and the gods, infuriated at this, imprisoned him in a magic net and bound him across three stones.

But Balder was condemned to die—and the first step had been taken towards Ragnarok, the day of doom when the gods will be overcome by the forces of evil. Balder, however, will survive the cataclysm. And after it a new world will arise, a green land inhabited by people who, like their ancient predecessors, will worship the shining god.

———— ❋ ————

SEA CREATURES

———— ❋ ————

SEDNA
North America (Inuit)

The Inuits of the Arctic regions feared Sedna more than any other deity and thought of her as gigantic, one-eyed, and hostile to humans. But she was not always like that. She had once been a mortal, a sweet and pretty maiden who lived by the sea with her widowed father, Angusta, until one day a kayak approached the shore. It was manned by a handsome young hunter holding an ivory spear and dressed in splendid furs. He wooed her with his song, imploring her to become his bride and follow him to the land of the birds, where there was never any hunger. He promised that he would give her ivory necklaces, soft bearskins to lie on, and a lamp always filled with oil.

Sedna finally yielded to his entreaties, entered his boat, and they sailed away. But too late, she found she had been deceived. Her seductive lover was not a real man but a bird-spirit. She was inconsolable. After a year, her father came to visit her. When he learned the truth and saw his daughter weeping in despair, he decided to take her away in his boat. Very soon a dark and terrible Arctic storm arose.

Angusta, realizing that he had angered the spirit, chose to sacrifice his daughter to save his own life. He thrust Sedna into the waves; but she clung desperately to the side of the boat. The cruel father then seized his ax and, one by one, cut off her clutching fingers, which at once became seals and whales. Eventually his daughter sank, but not before he had struck out one of her eyes.

Ever since, her heart full of hate for all humans, Sedna has ruled over the sea and the realm of the dead in the sea. As goddess of the sea creatures which are the Inuits' staple food, she must be placated in order to ensure success in hunting.

ALSO KNOWN AS: Nuliajuk Mother of Wild Life, Nerrivik the Food Dish

According to one legend, Sedna was the daughter of giants. She ate all the meat she could find, yet never had enough. When she attacked her parents to eat them too, they threw her into the sea after cutting off her fingers, and these became sea creatures.

WILD BEASTS

✳

ARTEMIS
Greece

The virgin goddess of the hunt and of the moon, and the twin sister of Apollo, the most beautiful of the gods of Olympus, Artemis matched her brother in beauty and, like him, was tall and imposing with golden curls.

Armed with a silver bow and deadly arrows made for her by Cyclopes, the one-eyed giant, she roamed the woods and mountainsides with her attendant nymphs, and here she hunted hinds and stags, lions and panthers.

Artemis was the child of Zeus and Leto, daughter of the Titans Phoebe and Croesus. She was born a day before her brother on the island of Ortygia. Immediately after her birth, she helped her mother to cross the narrow straits to Delos where she delivered her of Apollo— a foretaste of her role as protector of young children and patron of women in childbirth.

But Artemis was a goddess of contradictions. Although she protected women in labor, her swift arrows

ABOVE Even though this statue of Artemis is partly destroyed, it encapsulates the goddess' beauty.

LEFT The goddess confronts the pregnant Callisto before turning her into a bear.

OPPOSITE As goddess of the hunt Artemis carried a bow and a quiver full of arrows.

BELOW *The temple of Artemis at Brauron, near Athens. Noble Athenian maidens became members of her cult when they reached puberty, and were known as "bears" after one of her symbols. Many of the rites associated with the goddess were concerned with times of transition for women.*

LEFT *Artemis was an ancient goddess. This plaque dates from the seventh century* BC *and shows her in one of her early roles as "mistress of the animals."*

OPPOSITE *In this statue Artemis is surrounded by symbols of fertility; her many breasts reflect her connection with childbirth.*

also brought them sudden death. She was the guardian of suckling animals but gloried in the chase. And she was both a divinity of healing and the bringer of diseases like gout, rabies, leprosy, and malaria.

Above all, Artemis was associated with chastity. When she was three years old her father granted her wish for eternal virginity; all her companion nymphs were pre-pubertal nine-year-olds; and she exacted a fierce revenge on any man who approached her. When the hunter Actaeon inadvertently came upon her and her nymphs bathing naked in a woodland pool and paused to contemplate their beauty, the outraged goddess changed him into a stag and set his own pack of hounds to kill him. And when Orion, a giant and a great hunter, tried to rape her, she conjured up a scorpion that killed both him and his dog. Orion became a constellation and his dog was transformed into Sirius, the dog star.

The wrath of the goddess was also terrible when any of her companions gave in to love, however unwittingly. Although Callisto, one of her nymphs, allowed herself to be seduced by Zeus only because he approached her in the form of Artemis herself, the goddess changed her young companion into a bear and then shot her. Like Orion, Callisto was transported to the heavens, where she became the constellation of the Great Bear (also known as the Plough); the son she bore the great god was the ancestor of the Arcadians and possibly the twin brother of Pan.

Yet another legend describes how the goddess was enraged when Agamemnon, the hero who led the Greek forces in the war against Troy, had the effrontery to kill a stag in her sacred grove. To punish him she caused a dead calm to fall over the ocean and refused to raise the winds his ships needed in order to set sail for their destination until he had sacrificed Iphigenia, his daughter, to her.

Artemis' dark vindictiveness sits curiously with her earlier history as an orgiastic goddess, in whose honor men and women performed phallic dances; and this aspect of her personality is counterbalanced by her other, more beneficent aspects.

At Delphi, exquisitely attired, the beautiful goddess led the dances of the muses and graces. And when the moon shone, men's hearts, and even plants, rejoiced because it meant she was present.

She was also the bearer of light—a temple was erected to her in Athens harbor—and the patron of young Athenian maidens who, on reaching puberty, were initiated into her cult.

Many of the myths that surround Artemis were applied to Diana, the Roman goddess of woods, forests, and the moon, who was also the protector of virginity. Her name comes from Diviana, "the shining one."

Temples in her honor were erected on the shores of Lake Nemi, near Rome, and also in the city itself, where the most important was on the Aventine hill.

RICE

✸

INARI
Japan

As the rice god who ensures an abundant harvest of Japan's staple foodstuff, Inari is one of the most popular Japanese deities. He is also worshipped as the patron of agricultural prosperity and the god who brings

This statue is a traditional portrayal of Inari as bearded and carrying sheaves of rice—an image that links him closely to the farmers who worshipped him as a god of agriculture.

wealth and friends to households. His messenger and servant is the fox—which is itself endowed with supernatural powers—and on occasion, deity and animal merge to form one being. Inari is generally depicted as a bearded man sitting astride a white fox, and holding two sheaves of rice.

His shrines are found throughout Japan and are known as "fox shrines" because they contain images of these creatures. His temples, which are painted red, display a pear-shaped emblem and, like his shrines, have fox statues.

Inari occasionally changes gender and appears as a long-haired woman who, like her male counterpart, rides a white fox.

✸

CORN

✸

SELU (CORN WOMAN)
North America (Cherokee)

Selu, Corn Woman, and her husband Kanati, the lucky hunter, are at the heart of Cherokee culture. When Selu's twin sons, the Thunder Boys, see her producing corn by rubbing her stomach, they think she is a witch and plot to kill her. Selu, foreseeing this, asks them to clear a large plot of land first and drag her body around it seven times; instead they clear only seven small areas and drag her body around each twice. Where her blood falls the corn grows overnight, but many places remain where it cannot be cultivated.

✸

OPPOSITE This Navajo blanket depicts the maize plant, sacred throughout the new world.

MAIZE

YUM KAAX
Central America (Maya)

The Mayans of Central America worshipped a corn god, Yum Kaax, or "Lord of the Forests." Depicted as a handsome youth with a receding forehead and an ear of corn in his headdress, this deity also had a wider role as a guardian of agriculture.

Yum Kaax can be equated with the later Aztec god of maize, Cinteotl, to whom people offered their blood each April; reeds were dipped into it and displayed outside their houses to ensure a regular supply of food throughout the year.

LEFT Maize was an essential foodstuff, and Yum Kaax was a deity of agriculture as well as corn. This statuette shows him seated in a flower.

CHAPTER FIVE

※

FERTILITY

CHILDBIRTH

※

HATHOR
Egypt

The cow goddess Hathor is a complex deity; sometimes a daughter, sometimes a wife; protectress of women, childbirth, and the dead; queen of peace and love; queen of the palm tree and the sycamore; and mistress of music, dancing, and drinking. The Egyptians themselves found it difficult to define her role.

To all, however, she was a fertility goddess, the universal mother who brought forth the world, including the sun, Horus. Infant pharaohs were depicted as being suckled by her, and were called the sons of Hathor. The cow goddess was called on to assist at childbirth. But she also welcomed the dead to their new life in the underworld, giving them food

This unusual representation of the cow goddess Hathor shows her with a human head and a wig with curling plaits on each side of her cheeks, but with the ears of a cow.

※

and drink, and carrying them on her back to protect them from danger.

Hathor was shown in the form of a cow, or a woman wearing a crown of cow horns with a solar disk between them. Her sacred plant was the papyrus, which grows in the swamps by the Nile where wild cattle thrive. The rattle, or *sistrum*, was her sacred instrument, and the

※

Wedding of Bacchus, Roman counterpart of the Greek fertility god Dionysos, and Ariadne. Abandoned on the island of Naxos by her lover Theseus, the princess was rescued by the god.

columns of her temple at Dendera, her main sanctuary, were designed as *sistrums* in homage to her in her role as goddess of music, dancing, and sexual love.

On the first day of the new year, her priestesses climbed onto the roof terrace of the temple and presented her image to the rising sun, after which there was singing, dancing, and drinking. By contrast, in her role as an ideal mother figure Hathor was also connected with healing, and her temple housed the sick in mudbrick cubicles, where they were bathed in water from the sacred lake.

The cult of the cow goddess grew and extended far beyond Egypt. Her realm included the precious turquoise mines of the Sinai desert, and the rich province of Nubia which extended from Aswan to Khartoum. It was from there that Hathor sent the young Pepi II, of the sixth dynasty, her most magnificent gift on record: three hundred donkeys laden with ivory, gold, incense, ebony wood, and panther skins.

ALSO KNOWN AS: Hathyr, Athor, Athyr
IDENTIFIED WITH: Aphrodite

Hathor, also worshipped as a funerary goddess, is shown here in the form of a cow leaving the "western mountains" or underworld.

Hathor is shown here in her role as protectress of the dead. She is handing out refreshment from her seat in a sycamore tree to a priestess who, with her soul bird, is entering the underworld.

The cow goddess was the great nurturer and suckled pharaohs, and even humans, directly from her udders. This thirteenth-century BC relief is from a tomb in the Valley of the Kings.

CHILDBIRTH

FRIGG
Northern Europe

The second wife of Odin, the supreme deity of Norse mythology, Frigg was the "queen of heaven," the mother of Balder, the shining god, and of the blind Hoder.

A gentle fertility goddess, whose special spheres of influence were domestic contentment and happiness in marriage, she was a maternal deity—when Balder dreamt of impending calamity she was swift to extract oaths from all natural things, except the mistletoe, that they would not harm him—and she was invoked by women wanting children and during childbirth. But although she was

The gentle wife of Odin, the chief of the gods, Frigg was worshipped as the deity associated with family life and happiness.

revered as the consort of Odin, Frigg had not always been a faithful wife. Early in their marriage, when he left her to travel through the world, she enjoyed a liaison with his brothers

Ve and Vili, who had taken over his throne during his absence. Ull, the god of winter, archery, and skiing, was possibly another lover.

Nevertheless, she was the only deity in the Norse pantheon who was allowed to sit on Odin's great throne and, with him, see everything that was happening in the universe.

ALSO KNOWN AS: Frigga, Friya

EARTH MOTHER

PACHAMAMA
South America (Inca)

A goddess of fertility, Pachamama—the name means "earth mother"—was one of the lesser deities of the Inca pantheon. Inca astrological beliefs, which related the constellations to animals and birds, were closely connected with her cult: it was thought that the existence of the earthly forms of all these creatures depended on each of their celestial likenesses in the heavens.

One important constellation represented the llama, which was essential to the livelihood of the Inca villagers and was often sacrificed to Pachamama to ensure that the earth's fertility continued. Pachamama is still worshipped in some remote areas of the Andes.

IDENTIFIED WITH: The Virgin Mary

Demeter presents the gift of corn for mankind to Triptolemos, the son of the king of Eleusis. She is seated in a winged chariot.

FRUITS OF THE EARTH

DEMETER
Greece

The goddess of crops, vegetation, and fruit, and one of the most ancient of Greek deities, Demeter is the bringer of corn, which signifies civilization. Daughter of the Titans Cronos and Rhea, she was the sister of Zeus, Hades, Poseidon, and Hera. She was responsible for the seasons and also ensured plentiful harvests.

She had a daughter with Zeus, Persephone. Hades, lord of the underworld, fell desperately in love with his niece and one day, as she was picking flowers, he carried her away to his realm. Heartbroken, Demeter left Mount Olympus and, disguising herself as an old woman so that she would mingle more easily

plough, and her dragon-drawn chariot, and told him to take the art of agriculture to all mankind. To all those who had helped her, she gave the gift of corn. She then returned to Olympus, and fruitfulness returned to earth.

Her main feast, held in September, was a fertility rite from which men were excluded. Instead, pigs, snakes, pine cones, and other fertility symbols were thrown into her cave to regenerate the earth. Her attribute is an ear of corn.

Ceres, the Roman equivalent of Demeter, was a goddess of the fertile earth. She had a great following among the common people, and her festival, called Cerelia, was celebrated in the spring.

This first-century mosaic shows Ceres being worshipped in a temple on the Aventine hill in Rome. Games were held in her honor, and her popular festival, the Cerelia, took place in spring.

with mortals, wandered all over the world to find her daughter.

The king of Eleusis received her kindly, and entrusted his son Triptolemos into her care. But the land had become barren. Demeter was determined to withhold all grain until she saw her beloved daughter again. In order to restore world order, Zeus agreed with Hades that Persephone should return to earth at the first growth of spring, and remain there with her mother until the harvest was gathered in.

Demeter then revealed herself to the king of Eleusis and established a cult in his city. Her worshippers were initiated into mysterious rites, known as the Eleusinian Mysteries, that were alleged to convey the secret of the earth's fertility but which remain unknown to this day. To Triptolemos, Demeter gave seeds, a

SPRING

XIPE TOTEC
Central America (Aztec)

One of the most paradoxical of Aztec deities, Xipe Totec was the god of agriculture and vegetation. Every year he ensured a supply of food by allowing himself to be flayed alive, losing his skin in the same way that maize seeds lose theirs when they start to sprout. In winter a despised creature, diseased and in pain from sores and scabs, he reappeared after his sacrifice each spring as a splendid god, clad in green and wearing gold ornaments—a metaphor for the decay and renewal that is part of the cycle of the seasons. To celebrate the god's selfless action, men, women, and children were flayed during his festivals. One of these included ritual gladiatorial combats held between prisoners captured in war; the winners wore the rotting skins of the losers for twenty days.

The dark aspect of Xipe Totec is also reflected in the smallpox, plague, and blindness that he inflicted on mankind. His more beneficent side is shown in his patronage of workers in gold, the metal that most closely resembles ripening maize.

※

FERTILITY

※

LEGBA
Africa (Fon)

To the Fon people of Benin, Legba, the god of fertility and harvests, tends to be very mischievous. But he also knows the art of prophecy.

Very long ago, Legba lived with the supreme deity—usually referred to as God—and because he knew all the languages in the world, he acted as the divine messenger and executed God's orders. He was often reprimanded for playing tricks. But he became especially angry because he was always blamed for what went wrong, while God got the credit for what went right. So in revenge, he played a trick on his master. One dark and rainy night, he put on God's sandals and stole a large quantity of yams. Because of the sandal treads, God was blamed as the thief and was so upset that He went into a sulk and left the world.

Legba stayed behind and reported back to God every night. From Fa, who had sixteen eyes, he learned the secret of divining the

Fon religion was directed towards spirits called vodu, from which the name voodoo is derived. Shown here is a magic object: its spiked base indicates its link to the mischievous god Legba.

※

---

future—called "the house of sixteen doors." He soon had his own shrine in every house and every village.

To his devotees, he is a personal god. Outside each house stands a mound of clay from which protrudes a large phallus that represents Legba as master of the house. The small clay pots that surround it are always full of offerings of food, and the phallus is regularly anointed with oil and flour. When a chicken is sacrificed to the god, its feathers are stuck with its blood to the god's symbol.

※

FERTILITY

❋

FREY
Northern Europe

Frey and his twin sister Freya, the beautiful goddess of sexual love, were the children of the sea god Njord and the goddess Skadi. They were among the most celebrated of the Vanir, the early deities of the Norse pantheon who were concerned with imbuing the world with life and power. The most handsome of the gods, Frey was associated with summer, rain, and the sun, as well as with fertility. He helped and advised his worshippers, and a statue of him, attended by a priestess, was carried through the countryside to bless the changing seasons.

However, Frey also had his darker aspects: although he was regarded as god of peace, warriors wore his symbol—a boar's head—on their helmets during battle; horses—possibly even human beings—were sacrificed to him.

This detail from a twelfth-century tapestry shows Frey (right) holding an ear of corn. With him are Odin (left) and Thor (center).

Frey was the owner of a ship called Skipbladnir that flew through the air and was big enough to hold all the gods, yet small enough to fit into a pouch when it was folded up. With his sister Freya, he also owned a sacred boar, called Gullinborssti, with golden bristles that brought light to the world when it flew through the air.

Frey loved and married Gerda, a beautiful frost giantess, who at first refused even to consider him as a husband. She resisted a bribe of eleven of the golden apples that brought eternal youth to the gods, and the threat of being decapitated. She only agreed to marry Frey when the god's messenger threatened to curse her with unrequited lust, all-consuming hunger but no taste for food, and imprisonment at the gates of hell. Despite her initial reluctance, however, Gerda eventually came to love her husband and bore his son Fiolnir.

❋

FERTILITY

❋

DIONYSOS
Greece

The god of fertility, wine, and ecstasy, Dionysos, while still unborn, was saved from death by his father Zeus. The supreme god of ancient Greece rescued him from the flames that were consuming his mother, Semele—Hera's revenge on her philandering husband—and hid the unborn child in his thigh until he had become an adult.

Hounded by Hera, Dionysos wandered the world until he reached India, where he was

LEFT Dionysos rides a goat, symbol of fertility.

BELOW Dionysos with his vine and cornucopia is confronted by a mother and her twins.

tutored by Silenus, leader of the satyrs. He learned the use of the vine, and also of ivy which is both an intoxicant when chewed and a symbol of immortality.

Dionysos then returned to Greece. In unruly processions, riding or driving panthers, he crossed Asia with a tumultuous escort of satyrs, maenads—wild, drunken, and lustful women—and gods, and crossed the sea on a ship whose mast sprouted vine leaves. Captured by pirates, he changed them into dolphins. His followers indulged in orgiastic, drunken revelries, riotous dancing, and communal ecstasy. Respecting no laws or customs, Dionysos was chased, repressed, condemned, and attacked wherever he went. At last, he was accepted by Apollo at Delphi.

Worshipped as the great remover of inhibitions, Dionysos was a popular deity, particularly among women. Associated with wine and the release of natural impulses, his fertility cult was celebrated in secret mysteries or rites. During the spring festival, rituals reached paroxysms of frenzy, sometimes with both animals and humans being killed.

He was nevertheless a kind and generous god, often described as "the deliverer from cares." He gave King Midas his touch that turned everything into gold in return for helping a drunken satyr, and married Ariadne when she was abandoned by Theseus. Above all, Dionysos created wine, revered by the Greeks as a sacred drink, and made milk and honey flow.

His cult, associated with dancing, disguises, and wearing masks, gave birth to theater, drama, comedy, and satire. His attribute is a staff entwined with ivy.

Dionysos was known to the Romans as Bacchus, a corrupted epithet that means loud and rowdy. Unlike his Greek counterpart, Bacchus was solely a god of wine and drunkenness. His male followers were the satyrs. Women devotees were known as bacchae or bacchantes, and his ritual orgies were bacchanalia. The great mystic cult of Bacchus centered on wine, music, and dancing.

VIRILITY

CERNUNNOS
Celtic (Britain, Gaul)

Cernunnos, the "horned one" of Celtic mythology, was a mysterious figure who was worshipped throughout Britain and in what is now central France. A "lord of the animals," he wore the antlers of a stag or the horns of a ram—both symbols of virility—

Cernunnos was generally depicted with the beasts associated with his cult. The relief BELOW LEFT shows him with a bull and a stag; in the detail ABOVE, from the Gundestrup cauldron, the horned god's familiars include a snake, the symbol of rejuvenation.

and was also closely associated with two other creatures revered for their strength and pugnacity: the bull and the boar. The snake, representing rejuvenation, was another of his familiars and was sometimes shown with a ram's horns, doubly emphasizing the god's role as a deity of renewal and fertility.

But these were not his only responsibilities. A club-bearing figure carved into the hillside above Cerne Abbas in southwest England is thought to depict Cernunnos in his warlike as well as his virile aspects; and he is sometimes shown holding a purse, symbol of the wealth that was another of his concerns.

CHAPTER SIX

✵

LOVE, MARRIAGE, AND MOTHERHOOD

PLEASURE

✵

BASTET
Egypt

The goddess of pleasure and joy, and the symbol of sexual love, the cat goddess Bastet was approachable and caressable, and loved music and dancing. As the daughter of the sun god Re, she was mother of all the pharaohs, and their divine protector. She also gave protection against diseases and vermin. Her festival, celebrated with dancing and music, was the most magnificent in Egypt. It attracted huge crowds, and more wine was drunk then than in all the rest of the year.

Cats were sacred to Bastet and were themselves treated almost like deities. Killing one was punishable by death, and when a household pet died its family went into deep mourning and shaved their eyebrows. If a house caught fire, the first priority was to rescue the cat.

✵

Venus, the Roman goddess of love, was the Greek Aphrodite's counterpart. She is pictured here tenderly entwined with her son Cupid, the god of love.

✵

The cat goddess, shown here in a peaceful pose, was earlier represented as a ferocious lioness and said to be the sun god Re's instrument of vengeance.

✵

This veneration continued even after death: cat cemeteries throughout Egypt contained hundreds of thousands of cat corpses. All were mummified, with decorative designs and cat "faces," proof of the great love the Egyptians had for these animals, and for the goddess with whom they were associated. Her attribute was a sacred rattle.

ALSO KNOWN AS: Bast
IDENTIFIED WITH: Artemis

✵

DESIRE

EROS

Greece

Eros embodied the power of sex and amorous desire. He was blond and playful, a winged boy armed with a golden bow and arrows which he shot into the hearts of gods and mortals to awaken them to desire. He encouraged love between men and boys as a force that could move them to self-sacrifice—the Spartans honored him before battle. But he could be unscrupulous and often dangerous. He wounded hearts for fun, made people lose their reason or willpower, and showed no respect for age or station. At last, however, he himself fell in love—forever.

Eros was the son of Aphrodite, the goddess of love, and, always at his mother's side, he assisted her in her intrigues and affairs. Jealous of the beauty of the mortal Psyche, meaning "the soul," Aphrodite ordered him to make the maiden desire the ugliest man on earth. But Eros, disobeying his mother's command, fell in love with his intended victim and visited her every night although he remained invisible. Psyche returned his love and, unable to overcome her curiosity, lit a lamp to look at him while he was sleeping. A drop of hot oil awakened the god and, furious, he abandoned her.

Distraught, Psyche searched the world for her lover until Zeus took pity on her and the equally unhappy Eros, and gave his permission for them to marry.

Cupid, the Roman god of love—generally represented as the god of carnal love, holding a torch—was identified with Eros. A less powerful version of the Greek deity, he was one of the minor Roman gods. He was shown blindfolded, possibly to indicate that he chose his victims at random. The Romans also regarded him as a symbol of life after death and decorated sarcophagi with his image.

ALSO KNOWN AS: Amor

The poet Sappho described Eros as bitter-sweet: cruel to his victims, he was also charming and beautiful.

Eros, depicted as a young man on this Grecian vase, is about to release the fatal dart of desire from his golden bow. His wings indicate the speed of his action.

SEX

FREYA
Northern Europe

The twin sister of Frey, the Norse god of fertility, Freya was the most beautiful of all the goddesses and one of the most popular, not only with women who revered her for the help she gave them in marriage and childbirth, but also with warriors and kings: she often led the Valkyries, servants of Odin, to battlefields to select the slain heroes who would be allowed to enter Valhalla, the hall of the dead.

As the goddess of love and sex, she was also one of the most promiscuous of the deities. Although she shed tears of gold when her philandering husband Odur deserted her, she soon found solace in liaisons with a variety of suitors that included gods—even her brother Frey—elves, and mortal heroes.

Freya drove a chariot drawn by two cats and had the ability to change her shape, flying through the skies as a falcon or roaming the earth in the form of a she-goat.

She owned with Frey a golden boar whose bristles could light up the world, but her most treasured possession was the Brisingamen necklace, a piece of jewelry so beautiful that the goddess had prostituted herself to its four dwarf makers to obtain it. This infuriated Odin, one of her divine suitors, and he ordered the mischief-making Loki to steal the necklace and bring it to him. It was not an easy task: the trickster god first had to turn himself into a fly in order to creep into the impregnable fortress of Sessrymnir where Frey lived. Then, finding the goddess asleep in a position which did not allow him to take the

The most beautiful of the goddesses, Freya was renowned for her sexual liaisons; her lovers included human rulers whom she helped and advised.

Brisingamen, he was forced to change himself into a flea and bite her on her breast so that she turned over in her sleep, enabling him to unclasp the necklace.

When Freya discovered her loss and complained to Odin, the great god agreed to return the Brisingamen to her provided that she added the spreading of war to her other, more beneficent, responsibilities.

ALSO KNOWN AS: Freyja

AMOROUSNESS

KRISHNA
India

The eighth avatar of Vishnu, Krishna is the most popular of all the supreme deity's incarnations. To create him, the great god plucked out two of his own hairs, and placed a black one in the womb of the mother goddess Devaki, and a white one in that of Rohini, goddess of fortune. Krishna, who was dark skinned, was born from the black hair and his half-brother Balarama, who was fair, was born from the white one.

Krishna had both divine attributes and human failings. He was supremely heroic, yet could be deceitful and dishonest. He was a skilled musician—the very sound of his flute calmed storms and turbulent rivers—and renowned for his love of drink. Throughout his life he battled against the evil adversaries who threatened mankind. Yet he was also a womanizer who, despite his love for Radha whose golden beauty complemented his darkness, enjoyed many thousands of liaisons with other women.

In the *Bhagavad Gita,* Krishna is the charioteer of Arjuna, a warrior, and in the course of the epic poem he reveals his godlike nature to him. In another text, he embodies the universe.

Although Krishna's good looks enchanted more than a thousand women, his consort and true love was the golden-skinned milkmaid Radha. The illustration ABOVE shows the couple standing on a lotus flower; the god is playing a flute, one of his attributes. The eighteenth-century painting RIGHT shows them in a grove by the River Jumna; the god is wearing a kingly crown.

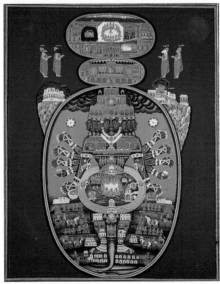

ABOVE Krishna holds Mount Govardhana above local people to protect them and their cattle from a great deluge. He had persuaded his herdsman foster father to stop worshipping Indra and the god had sent the flood as punishment for this act of disloyalty. As a result of Krishna's feat in supporting the mountain, Indra recognized that the youth was the lord of cattle.

LEFT This shows Krishna in cosmic form; many-headed and with ten arms, he is all-seeing and all-powerful. He towers above the earthly world and the symbols he holds in his hands include a conch shell and lotus flowers. This is a relatively modern illustration; traditionally the god, in his role as the embodiment of the cosmos, is shown with the sky as his eyes, heaven as his navel and the stars as his chest.

*Krishna defeated the water serpent
Kaliya by dancing on its head.
He spared the monster's life and
promised that it would be safe
from Garuda, the enemy of all
snakes—but banished it from river
waters to the depths of the ocean.*

He grew up in a herdsman's family, but even as a child his supernatural abilities were apparent: he sucked the life out of Putana, a female demon, and uprooted two trees to which he had been tethered.

As a young man he fought and killed demons with his half-brother Balarama, obtained the discus that belonged to the fire god Agni, killed the serpent Kaliya, and—the ultimate aim of his incarnation—defeated the evil King Kamsa who had usurped his kingdom of Mathura, and so saved the world.

Krishna himself died as the result of an accident when a hunter called Jaras or "old age" mistook him for a deer and shot him in his right heel—his one vulnerable spot.

Krishna is sometimes shown with Garuda, the divine sun bird and enemy of serpents, who was also Vishnu's mount. His color is black or dark blue and his attributes include a flute, a staff, and a prayer wheel.

ALSO KNOWN AS: Krsna

SEXUAL LOVE

✤

XOCHIQUETZAL
Central America (Aztec)

Xochiquetzal—most precious flower—a young, beautiful, and alluring deity, was a Central American goddess who brought the Aztec world sexual love, pleasure, and fecundity. Her other responsibilities were a natural extension of these concerns: protecting women when they were pregnant and in childbirth, and caring for young mothers; ensuring that the earth was fruitful with crops and flowers; and overseeing all handicrafts—weavers regarded her as their special patron.

Her powers had been greatest during the reign of the beneficent god Quetzalcoatl in Toltec times, when she graced the whole world with fruitfulness and flowers, and when marigolds were offered to her at festivals of the dead. But after Quetzalcoatl's defeat by his dark adversary Tezcatlipoca, Xochiquetzal was less active and bounteous. It was therefore vital for the Aztecs to honor her, and young women on the verge of matrimony braided their hair into a likeness of two of the quetzal plumes that were sacred to her.

Elaborate rituals were performed in order to propitiate her. Each year a beautiful young girl was chosen to impersonate her, and was ritually married to a youth who impersonated the dark god Tezcatlipoca. On the day of Xochiquetzal's festival, lavish celebrations were held by the master craftspeople of the Aztec capital Tenochtitlan—metalworkers, sculptors, painters, weavers, embroiderers, and workers in feathers—who presented the impersonator to the goddess. The young girl was sacrificed and flayed by Xochiquetzal's priests, and a young man donned her skin and an elaborate costume. He sat at a loom and pretended to weave, while the craftspeople, clothed as animals like jaguars, dogs, and monkeys, danced around him. Then all confessed their sins to the goddess and atoned by slashing their tongues. In this way the Aztec people ensured their survival into the future.

Although Xochiquetzal was a goddess of love and pleasure she, like other Aztec deities, demanded human sacrifice. This wooden effigy, a rare survival of pre-conquest Aztec art, depicts her as a young and beautiful woman.

LOVE

✳

APHRODITE
Greece

Aphrodite, the daughter of Zeus and the nymph Dione, was the goddess of love and beauty. She reigned over the hearts and senses of all men, gods and mortals alike.

All women were her rivals, her pawns, her worshippers, and even her slaves.

According to one legend, she was born fully grown but naked out of the *aphros* or foam that formed when the Titan Cronos castrated his hated father Uranus, and threw the phallus into the sea where it floated in white foam and engendered Aphrodite. The zephyrs carried her to Cythera, and from there to Cyprus where she was clothed and covered in perfume and jewels, then taken to the gods. Her beauty was perfect. She was the embodiment of charm, seduction, and sensuality. She was also jealous, cruel, and promiscuous. She married Hephaistos, the lame and ugly god of fire, on Zeus' orders, but she was soon unfaithful and had innumerable lovers.

Aphrodite's liaison with Ares, the god of

The Hellenistic marble ABOVE shows Aphrodite, the Venus of Rhodes, bathing. The beauty and reputation of the goddess of love have inspired artists around the world. In the painting RIGHT, she attempts to hold back Adonis as he prepares to hunt the wild boar that will kill him.

RIGHT Although the goddess of love was one of the earliest of the Greek deities, her worship continued into the Christian era and beyond. This mosaic dates from the third century AD.

BELOW A portrayal of the birth of Aphrodite in its most popular version: she emerged naked and fully grown from the foam of the sea waves and was carried by the zephyrs, seen here as winged cherubs, to the island of Cythera. According to Homer, however, the goddess was the daughter of Zeus and Dione, a sea nymph.

RIGHT *Aphrodite is believed to have originated in West Asia and to be the Greek version of Astarte, an oriental goddess of love and fertility. This third-century* BC *terracotta statuette of Aphrodite is from Myrina in Asia Minor (modern Anatolia).*

LEFT *This graceful statuette from the Hellenistic period represents Aphrodite in an untypically modest pose. It is made of bronze and encrusted with silver.*

BELOW *A mosaic from Tunisia portrays Aphrodite preparing to dress her hair with the assistance of two winged infants.*

war—who fathered Eros—could have been dangerous. Hephaistos caught them making love, bound them in his magic net, and exposed them, as they were, to the full assembly of Olympian gods. He asked for just retribution, but instead the gods roared with laughter, and the couple went free.

Hermes, Dionysos, and Poseidon were among her divine lovers. But the love of her life was Adonis, the beautiful son of the king of Syria and his daughter Myrrha. The goddess was so totally seduced by the young man that she followed him everywhere, and was no longer to be seen in heaven. When he was killed by a wild boar, in spite of her warnings, the goddess was inconsolable. It is said that each tear she shed for her young lover turned into a rose.

In order to be judged the most beautiful goddess by Paris, Aphrodite promised him Helen's hand—and brought about the Trojan war. The power and determination of the love goddess is apparent in this bronze head.

The goddess of love caused suffering as well as pleasure. One of her great rivals was Hera, consort of Zeus, and to spite her Aphrodite forced Zeus to make love to mortal women and neglect his wife. Zeus retaliated by forcing Aphrodite to fall in love with a poor, simple—and mortal—shepherd called Anchises. From this union came Aeneas, founder of the Latin nation. Anchises fared less well. To punish him for having dared to sleep with a goddess,

Aphrodite sent a swarm of bees to blind him, while Zeus made him lame with a well-aimed thunderbolt.

Her main shrines were in Cyprus, Cythera, and Corinth, where she was worshipped by young girls who lived in her temples and sacrificed their virginity to the goddess by offering themselves to passers-by. When these rites later became associated with prostitution, slaves were employed in order to perform them.

Aphrodite is portrayed in countless sculptures that celebrate the perfection of her form, and paintings illustrating the legends that are attached to her name. Her attribute is a dove, the symbol of love.

Venus was Aphrodite's Roman counterpart, and was the deity of gardens, spring, and fruitfulness before she was worshipped as the goddess of love and beauty. Through her son Aeneas she was regarded by the Romans as the founder of their race.

An important figure in the official state cult—Julius Caesar and Nero claimed to be her descendants—she was the protectress of the Roman people. Many temples were erected in the name of Venus, and the goddess of love was represented on numerous coins.

VOLUPTUOUSNESS

❈

KAMA
India

Kama, the Hindu god of love, was the first deity to be born. He sprang directly from the heart of the creator god Brahma and, as the embodiment of carnal desire, he was a powerful force from the very start of creation. His consorts were Rati, the goddess of sexual desire and affection, and Priti, the goddess of pleasure; Vasanta, the god of spring, was a close companion; and nymphs were his attendants. Beautiful and brilliant, he rode on an elephant or bird, and was armed with a bow made from sugar cane and strung with honey bees; its flower-tipped arrows could induce anyone they pierced to fall in love.

One of these arrows cost Kama his handsome form when Indra, the god of war, commanded him to fire it at Shiva the destroyer, who was deep in meditation, to arouse him and fill him with desire for the goddess Parvati, daughter of King Himalaya. Shiva's anger at being disturbed was so great that lightning flashed from his middle eye and burnt Kama to cinders. Although the god of love was reborn, his body could not be restored to him and he now bears the epithet *ananga* or "bodiless."

Kama's chief festival, Madonatsava, was once a celebration of song, dance, and sexual desire. Today he is invoked by brides when they leave their family homes; and his name is commemorated in the *Kama Sutra,* a classic treatise on erotic technique. His attributes are a bow and arrows, and ornaments.

❈

MARRIAGE

❈

HERA
Greece

Hera was the sister and wife of Zeus, and the queen of heaven. The ultimate personification of womanhood, she was the goddess of marriage and the protector of childbirth, the home, and the family.

She was also jealous and quarrelsome. She pursued the mistresses, divine or mortal, of her adulterous husband with a cruel vengeance, torturing and killing them and persecuting their children, often with dramatic results for gods, heroes, and men. She put two enormous snakes in the cradle of the newborn Heracles, and held Io under the guard of Argus of the hundred eyes. And she did not hesitate to wipe out the city of Troy simply because Paris, the

Hera had many sanctuaries where temples were dedicated to each stage of a woman's life. This one is at Olympia.

son of Priam, the city's king, had judged Aphrodite to be more beautiful than she.

Never once unfaithful to her husband, she nonetheless succeeded in conceiving by herself, out of desire or hate. Some of her best-known children were produced when she slapped the ground with her hand or ate a lettuce. Among them were the monster Typhon, alone capable of overpowering Zeus; Hephaistos, lame and ugly; Ares, the violent god of war; and Hebe, the goddess of youth.

Hera was venerated by women, who relied on her to make their marriages happy, long-lasting, and fruitful. Argos was the center of her cult, and she was generally worshipped in high places: most of her temples were built on mountaintops. She carries a scepter and wears a diadem, and her sacred animals are the peacock and the cow.

Juno, Hera's Roman counterpart, was also a goddess of fecundity: her month, June, was considered the most favorable for weddings. But her most important role was as protector of the whole Roman Empire. Her flock of sacred geese were kept in the Capitol.

WIFE

LAKSHMI
India

Lakshmi, the lotus goddess of prosperity and abundance, is the wife of Vishnu in his many incarnations. As Sita, she was the consort of Rama, abducted by the demon Ravana; as Padma she emerged from a lotus to sit beside him when he was the dwarf Vamana;

and she was first the cowgirl Rada and then the goddess Rukmini to his Krishna. Whatever her form, she is always the faithful and subservient companion of the great god.

She arose from the primal ocean which the gods, under the leadership of Vishnu, churned until the water turned to milk and then to butter and gave birth to the sun and moon, the goddess and, ultimately, the elixir of immortality. Because of her association with the act of creation, she is also the universal mother.

Lakshmi is golden, the color of the lotus, and full breasted. She wears lotus garlands around her neck and is usually shown sitting or standing on a lotus flower. During her festival of Divali, held in late October or early November, her worshippers light lamps to honor one of Hinduism's most beautiful and attractive goddesses.

ALSO KNOWN AS: Laksmi, Shri

Lakshmi, the wife and universal mother and the constant consort of Vishnu, stands on a lotus and holds its flowers in her hands.

MOTHERHOOD

KWAN YIN
China

Kwan Yin, the deity to whom newly married couples pray for children, was the youngest daughter of a king of Thailand. A virtuous maiden, she took a vow of virginity and resisted her father when he insisted that she should marry. He angrily and reluctantly allowed her to enter a Buddhist convent, but only on condition that she washed and cooked for the whole community of five hundred nuns. She was helped in this impossible task by the gods, who took pity on her and performed her duties for her; this aroused the wrath of her father who set fire to the convent in his fury. When she quelled the flames with miraculous powers, her father attempted to behead her; but his sword broke, so he strangled her instead. When she arrived in the realms of the dead, she recited the holy books and her powers were so great that the rulers of the underworld were unable to apportion punishments to evildoers. They sent her back to the world where, because of her great spiritual wisdom, she was made immortal by the Buddha. Meanwhile, her father had succumbed to a disease so terrible that it could be cured only by medicine made from the hands and eyes of a living person. She allowed her hands to be cut off and her eyes gouged out so that he could be made well again. When he recovered, he saw the error of his ways, was converted to Buddhism and left his kingdom—while his daughter was miraculously made whole again.

ABOVE Mothers and would-be mothers offer special prayers to Kwan Yin, a goddess so pure that when her father insisted that she should marry, she tended a community of 500 Buddhist nuns rather than obey him. This marble statue dates from the Tang Dynasty and shows her seated on a lotus flower, a symbol of purity.

LEFT Compassionate and merciful, Kwan Yin has long elicited unprecedented devotion in China and is invoked by her devotees when danger threatens. Despite the cruel treatment she endured from her father she sacrificed her eyes and hands to cure him when he was dying.

RIGHT The many arms of Kwan Yin in this image symbolize the extent of her intercessory powers. The goddess is invoked by prisoners desperate to lose their shackles and as a bodhisattva, an "enlightened being," she helps men and women to attain deliverance.

BELOW This magnificent image of Kwan Yin from the Kek Lok Si temple in Penang reflects her serenity. The goddess is shown with a halo and holds a willow branch, symbol of beauty in her hand. Her many powers include the ability to drain snakes of their venom.

Kwan Yin, through her compassion and purity, elicits a devotion unmatched by any other deity. She gives help and guidance freely and liberally with no need for recompense, and receives none of the usual offerings of food and wine. Not only do young couples pray to her for children and pregnant women for sons, but mothers invoke her for the well-being of their sons and daughters, and prisoners ask her help to escape their shackles. She can remove venom from snakes and even quell the power of lightning. Depicted haloed and sitting on a lotus, symbol of purity, she holds

Kwan Yin has never asked for offerings and libations, and extends her help and guidance gladly to those who need it.

a vase filled with the dew of compassion and a willow branch, an emblem of beauty. She is often shown with many arms, symbolizing the extent of her intercessory powers.

ALSO KNOWN AS: Kuan Yin, Kwannon, Guanyin

MOTHERHOOD

PARVATI
India

The mother goddess of Hindu mythology, Parvati was the gentle wife of Shiva the destroyer and ascetic, and the mother of two deities: Ganesha, the elephant-headed god of good fortune, and Skanda, a god of war. The daughter of Himalaya, the mountain king, and Mena, sister of Vishnu, she fell in love with Shiva as a young girl but, despite her great beauty, he spurned her because of her dark color. Although Kama had pierced him with an arrow of desire while he was meditating on a mountaintop, Shiva merely incinerated the god of love and returned to his contemplations.

To demonstrate her devotion, Parvati practiced such rigorous self-denial that her body glowed with a golden hue. She finally won Shiva's love and, as his consort, ensures that the energy engendered by his asceticism is channeled to earth for the benefit of mankind.

Parvati is depicted with two or four arms, and is sometimes shown embracing Shiva, or with him and their two sons. Her attributes include a conch shell, rosary, crown, and mirror, and her mount is a lion.

LEFT Parvati and Shiva relax in their home high in the Himalayas, with their sons the elephant-headed Ganesha, god of good fortune, and Skanda, a god of war.

ABOVE Parvati is the epitome of the devoted wife and mother, and one of Hinduism's most popular goddesses. This temple is in northern India.

CHAPTER SEVEN

HOUSEHOLD

GATEWAYS

JANUS
Rome

Janus, son of the sun god Apollo, had two faces that looked in opposite directions. All gateways and doorways were sacred to him: he holds a janitor's staff in his left hand and keys in his right hand when acting as a guardian of exits and entrances. The god frustrated a treacherous plot to betray Rome to the Sabines, and from then on his double-doored temple on the forum, which was kept locked in peacetime, was opened at times of war to allow him out to protect the city. First in the list of gods to be invoked by the Romans in prayer, he was also responsible for bringing agriculture and law to mankind.

The god of past, present, and future, his two faces could be seen as symbolizing either failure

This Roman coin clearly shows the two faces of Janus, the god of gateways and beginnings, and of the 365 days of the year, who symbolized both possible aspects of the future: success or failure.

Ganesha, the Hindu god of good fortune, was the son of Parvati and Shiva the destroyer. One of India's most popular gods, his worshippers invoke him before setting out on a journey or starting an enterprise.

or success, and his role extended to beginnings in general: sunrise, sunset, and each new season. His principal feast was at the start of each new year—the month of January, which began the Roman year, was named after him—and he is often depicted holding the number 365, representing the days of the year.

Symbolism loomed large in the worship of Janus, not least at his temple in Rome which was constructed to a symmetrical design: it was a perfect square, each side with four doors symbolizing the four seasons and with three windows, collectively standing for the twelve months of the year.

Janus' influence continues to this day: January I remains an important time for looking both forwards and back and a gateway for good resolutions.

GUARDIAN

HEIMDALL
Northern Europe

Heimdall was the guardian of Asgard, where the gods resided, a tireless sentry whose senses were so acute that he could see in the dark and hear grass growing. He lived beside the rainbow-bridge of Bifrost that linked the home of the gods to the rest of the world. His task in Norse mythology is to alert his fellow deities to invasion by the frost giants and the coming of Ragnarok, their day of doom, by blowing on his trumpet, known as the Gjallarhorn.

He was the son of nine giant mothers, who were the waves of the sea; but despite his unusual parentage he was wise, beautiful, and good. He enjoyed wandering through earthly realms and was the progenitor of three classes of human beings: serfs, peasants, and members of the ruling class. Each of these was the result of Heimdall's dalliance with a different mortal woman. Serfs were the descendants of the god's son Thrall, a strong and willing

---

Heimdall, lived beside a rainbow bridge that linked Asgard, with the earthly world. He fathered three classes of human beings: rulers, peasants, and serfs.

Heimdall repels an attack by dragons. As the guardian of Asgard he will warn the gods of the coming of Ragnarok; and die after killing his old enemy Loki, the trickster deity.

worker. Peasants were the children of Karl, a farmer; and warriors and rulers, including the first king of Denmark, were descended from the god's most handsome son, Jarl.

Heimdall fought and won a mighty battle with the mischief-making Loki; a contest that will be repeated at Ragnarok, when the guardian deity of Asgard will kill the trickster god—and die.

GUARDIANS OF THE FAMILY

DOMOVOY
Russia and Slav Lands

Each household in Russia, and throughout the Slav lands of Eastern Europe, lived, according to tradition, under the protection of a Domovoy, a household spirit who hid in unexpected corners of the home, near the fireplace or under the doorstep. Today they are still worshipped in parts of Siberia. By origin an ancestral spirit, each Domovoy takes it upon himself to guard the family and all its possessions—but only as long as they are industrious and clean-living, and provided they leave out supplies of his favorite food every night. Any breaches of this strict code are punished with loud knocks and groans; plates are smashed and farm animals tormented.

A troublesome Domovoy has to be placated with special meals, and by being introduced to new farm animals which must be the color he prefers. As he can foresee the future, his groans, grunts, and cries are carefully analyzed by his family as portents of good or evil. Usually invisible, he sometimes appears in the form of a gray-haired old man, perhaps covered with fur. At times, too, he brushes against members of his family; a soft touch signifies good luck while a hard, cold contact presages death or ill fortune. When a family moves, its members entice their Domovoy to come with them by performing elaborate rituals—which may include offering him coals from the old hearth.

HOME

THE LARES AND PENATES
Rome

Every Roman household relied on the Lares and Penates to protect its home and its family. The Lares were pairs of dancing youths, each of whom held a wreath or a horn. They

The Lares, guardians and protectors of homes and families, were depicted as youths carrying wreaths of flowers or horns in their hands.

HEARTH

VESTA
Rome

Vesta, the special goddess of the hearth and fire, was worshipped in every Roman house, generally in the form of a strikingly beautiful woman holding a votive bowl and lighted torch.

She was the special protectress of Rome, and the sacred flame—the hearth of the city itself—burnt in her circular temple in the

The temple of Vesta in the forum at Rome contained the goddess' sacred flame, the hearth of the city. The fire was guarded by vestal virgins who ensured that it burned continuously and was never extinguished.

resided in small shrines in the corner of the main room of each house, and were honored with daily prayers and offerings. They were also patrons of travelers, ensuring them a safe return, and protected people from danger at crossroads.

The Penates were first the guardians of the store cupboard, but extended their sphere to the hearth which they shared with the Lares; like them, they received daily offerings from their households. For even the most sophisticated Romans, the Lares and Penates were therefore both guardians and guides and an embodiment of "home sweet home."

forum. It was attended by six vestal virgins, usually of royal or noble blood, who wore white wedding gowns with purple edging. They were bound for thirty years by a solemn vow of chastity, and any violations were punished with the ultimate severity: the erring virgin would be buried alive.

The first day of Vesta's festival, June 9, heralded a time of bad luck. Married women would process barefoot to her temple with offerings of food; and asses—sacred to the goddess because one was said to have helped her to repulse the unwelcome advances of the fertility god Priapus—were decorated with wreaths. Once the vestal virgins had swept out her temple and deposited the rubbish in the River Tiber on June 15, life in Rome returned to normal.

IDENTIFIED WITH: Hestia

FIRE

AGNI
India

The Hindu god of fire, and the very personification of the element itself, Agni is both beneficent and awesome. As a natural force he brings warmth and light to mankind, but in his destructive aspect he can be terrible: the *Mahabharata*, the sacred book of the Hindus and the world's longest epic, describes how the fire god, exhausted from consuming too many offerings of clarified butter, renewed his vigor by devouring an entire forest.

With Indra, the god of rain and war, and the sun god Surya, Agni is one of the three chief deities invoked in the *Rig Veda*, the ancient collection of Hindu hymns.

He lives on earth and intercedes with the gods on behalf of human beings, and carries sacrificial offerings to them in the form of fire. And when men and women die he gives them immortality and cleanses them of sin, consuming their bodies as they lie on their funeral pyres and conveying them to the other-worlds of ghosts and ancestors. Agni has more modest duties; he is the domestic fire that is at the center of every household, and is also the fire of passion.

Because of his earthly connections, Agni is associated with *soma*, an intoxicating drink that was made from a hallucinogenic plant and used in early sacrificial rituals.

This bronze statuette of Agni shows the god in human form. He is associated with light and warmth and with the life-giving heat of the sun but, like fire itself, he can also be a destructive force.

Legends describe him as the son of the creator god Dyaus, as being born from the sun, lightning, or water—or from a lotus that had been created by Brahma, the wise creator god. His consort is Svadha, daughter of a sun god. He has two faces and is bearded, red in color, and clothed in fire, with seven tongues to lick up the butter that is offered to him in daily Brahman rituals.

The god of fire is often portrayed riding a goat or driving a chariot drawn by parrots or red horses. His attributes are flames, a trident, and a water pot.

IDENTIFIED WITH: Shiva the destroyer

Bes was the protector of the household. Because his ugliness was believed to frighten away evil spirits, he was always represented full face, whether on bas-reliefs as BELOW or the faience kohl pot RIGHT.

HUMAN PLEASURES

BES
Egypt

Egypt's most popular household deity was a lecherous, rude and comical dwarf called Bes. Fond of music, singing, and drinking, he was associated with all the human pleasures. He brought prosperity to married couples, encouraged lovemaking, assisted in childbirth, and watched over children. His image was in every home, carved on bedposts and mirrors and painted on bedroom walls—even those of royal bedrooms.

Bes had a large bearded face, wide projecting ears, and a protruding tongue. Plump and bowlegged, he wore a leopard or lion skin which still had its tail, and an ostrich feather in his uncombed hair. Because his ugliness was thought to deter evil spirits, Bes the protector,

unlike all other Egyptian deities who were painted only in profile, was always pictured full face. His attributes are musical instruments—to ward off evil spirits—and knives.

Although he was primarily a guardian deity, he was also god of cosmetics and all forms of female ornament and was depicted on kohl tubes, rouge pots, and perfume flasks.

When Egypt fell to the Romans, in about 31 BC, the occupying forces adopted this genial god, and adapted his Egyptian dress to that of a legionary.

ALSO KNOWN AS: Besu, Bisu

✳

GOOD LUCK

✳

FORTUNA
Rome

At first the enhancer of harvests and flocks and a helper to women in childbirth, Fortuna developed a wider role as the Roman goddess of good fortune. She personified luck and spoke through oracles. Slaves, who were normally excluded from religious celebrations and rites, were allowed to attend her festival on June 11—as good fortune was seen as having no respect for rank or status.

The daughter of Jupiter, Fortuna was depicted with a helmsman's rudder which enabled her to steer fate; a cornucopia, from which plenty could flow; and a globe that symbolized chance. But the most enduring image of the goddess was her wheel: a reminder that luck may not last.

✳

Fortuna holds a helmsman's rudder and a cornucopia or horn of plenty, from which good luck could flow. Originally a goddess who was especially concerned with women, she became the personification of luck.

LONG LIFE

✳

SHOU LAO
China

Originally identified with the star Canopus, the second brightest in the heavens which ensured peace when it could be seen from earth, Shou Lao came to control the destiny of all mankind. As the president of the department of heavenly administration, responsible to the Great Emperor of the

Eastern Peak, he fixes each person's time of death by inscribing it on a tablet at the time of their birth: only on very rare occasions can the anguished entreaties of the parents induce him to change his mind. Worshipped as part of people's birthday celebrations, he is usually shown smiling, holding a peach, and with a white crane or a turtle, both attributed with remarkable longevity.

ALSO KNOWN AS: Shou Hsing, Shou Xing Lao Tou Zi, Nan-Ji Xian-Weng

Ts'ai Shen offers special gifts of riches to men and women who are prepared to admit him to their homes—and greet him with the reverence he demands—during the first days of the new year.

WEALTH

TS'AI SHEN
China

During the first days of the new year, Chinese families worship Ts'ai Shen, god of riches, who appears as a visitor bringing gifts for those willing to admit him to their homes and offer him due reverence. The god of mandarins, he presides over an elaborate division of the ministry of wealth. Identified with different historical personalities, in one account he was originally a hermit whose supernatural powers allowed him to ride on a tiger. Ts'ai Shen is depicted wearing a pink robe—reminiscent of spring and the force of Yin, the feminine principle—with a ring of coins around its hem. He has a lotus motif, a symbol of fertility, on his chest and carries a golden mushroom denoting longevity.

ALSO KNOWN AS: Cai Shen, Ts'ai Shen Yeh

SLEEP

HYPNOS
Greece

Hypnos, the Greek god of sleep, was orig-inally a man who took on the form of a bird and tricked Zeus, the supreme deity, into sleep. This aroused the great god's wrath. Hypnos, terrified, fled from the earth. He sought refuge with Nyx, god of night, and became divine. He inhabited the underworld by day and never saw the sun; but at night he came out into the world to bring sleep to mankind, brushing the foreheads of insomniacs with a branch or gently pouring sleep-inducing liquid from a horn.

Hypnos had three sons. While Morpheus brought dreams to human beings, Phobetor and Phantasos did the same for animals and inanimate objects. Thanatos, Hypnos' brother, helped those who were weary of life to die.

Known to the Romans as Somnus, Hypnos was depicted as a winged youth holding a horn and a poppy.

※

SUCCESS

※

GANESHA
India

Short and pot-bellied, with the head of an elephant, Ganesha is the deity who removes obstacles and brings good fortune to his worshippers. His animal appearance is the result of an argument between his parents, Shiva the destroyer and Parvati, the constant wife and deity concerned with fertility and motherhood. The goddess created her son from skin that flaked off her body while she was bathing and, in need of a protector, asked him to guard her rooms against intruders. This the boy did, even against his father, who was so infuriated at being barred from his wife that he accidentally decapitated him. Parvati was distraught and the god, to placate her, replaced her son's head with that of the first creature he saw: an elephant.

Ganesha has only one tusk, a reflection of his roles as patron of the art of writing and "lord of learning;" it is said that he broke off the other in order to write down the 110,000 couplets of the *Mahabharata,* the world's longest epic poem.

A gentle deity, Ganesha is one of the most popular gods in the Hindu pantheon. He is invoked at the start of journeys and important enterprises and is especially loved by students. Yellow in color, he rides on a rat, and has four arms in which he carries a shell, a discus, a water lily, and a club.

ALSO KNOWN AS: Ganesa

This statue portrays the elephant-headed Ganesha in traditional style: short and pot-bellied with four hands; the rat on the plinth is a familiar attendant.

KITCHEN

※

TSAO CHUN
China

Tsao Chun, god of the kitchen, probably originated as prince of the furnace—*tsao* means hearth, or furnace—in the Han Dynasty. He is generally portrayed as a kind old gentleman surrounded by his wife and children; yet his role is more that of Big Brother. From his "temple," a small niche by the cooking stove where he is represented by a paper picture, he records the family's every move and every word.

Then on the night of the twenty-fourth day of the twelfth moon, Tsao Chun ascends to

---
※

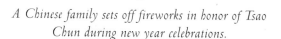

A Chinese family sets off fireworks in honor of Tsao Chun during new year celebrations.

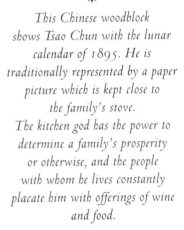

This Chinese woodblock shows Tsao Chun with the lunar calendar of 1895. He is traditionally represented by a paper picture which is kept close to the family's stove. The kitchen god has the power to determine a family's prosperity or otherwise, and the people with whom he lives constantly placate him with offerings of wine and food.

heaven to make his report to the August of Jade, supreme ruler and patron of the Chinese emperors, who lived in a palace and was served by a bureaucracy of deities and celestial beings. The household's prosperity, or adversity, depends upon his statement. Therefore, in order to sweeten his tongue, offerings of paper money, honey cakes, and wine are made to him. His image is burned on a small fire of pine wood, and then fireworks are sent off to light his ascension.

When the god returns to earth, a new paper image is placed in the niche, where it remains throughout the year. During Tsao Chun's absence, members of the family are free to do as they please. But they always remember that disaster may strike without his protection.

CHAPTER EIGHT

ARTS AND CRAFTS

ALL SKILLS

LUG
Celtic (Ireland)

Lug was the god of all the arts and crafts, a wise man, a sorcerer, and a musician. Above all, however, he was the divine warrior who led the Tuatha Dé Danann, the gods of light and goodness, to victory over the Formarians, grotesque and violent giants who represented all that was evil and sinister in ancient Ireland.

As an infant, Lug had narrowly escaped death at the hands of his grandfather, a leader of the Formarians who was known as Balor of the Evil Eye because of the malevolence of his gaze which could overpower an army of men. Believing a prophecy that he would be killed by his own grandson, Balor had imprisoned his only daughter in a cave. When she was nevertheless seduced, Balor attempted to

Lug led the forces of good to victory against the evil Formarians in one of the great battles of Irish mythology. This Celtic head is probably a representation of the god.

drown the triplets to whom she gave birth. But Lug was rescued and, fostered by the smith god Goibhnu, grew up to be a handsome and brilliant young man.

On the eve of the final battle between the Tuatha Dé Danann and the Formarians, as the forces of good gathered at the palace of Tara, Lug gained admittance to their king, Nuanda, by claiming that he was skilled in all the arts—those of a poet, physician, historian, harpist, hero, and many more. Persuaded by

This detail from a painting by Rubens shows Hephaistos, the Greek smith god, in his forge. He was the patron of those who used fire in their trades.

his abilities, Nuanda gave him his throne and allowed him to prepare for the battle. Lug deployed the forces of good—druids, craftsmen, and sorcerers as well as warriors—with such skill that the Formarians were defeated. During the battle he killed his grandfather by piercing his eye with a sling stone.

Lug was the lover of Déchtire, the daughter of a druid; their son Cúchulainn was one of the great heroes of Irish mythology, renowned for his strength and beauty.

There is a tradition that Lug was last seen in the second century AD when he appeared to the high king, Conn of a Hundred Battles, and told him the length of his reign and how many children he would have. Long before then, however, Lug and the other old gods had been conquered by the ancestors of the Gaels and forced to live underground. Over the centuries, the potency of the god of all skills dwindled until he became nothing more than a fairy craftsman—*Lugh-chromain* or "little stooping Lug"—a name that has entered the English language as that creation of Irish folklore: a leprechaun. His attributes are the spear and the sling.

ALSO KNOWN AS: Lug, Lugus, Lynx

MEDICINE
✳
SUKUNA-BIKO
Japan

The Japanese god of medicine traveled throughout the world and knew all there was to know about it. His knowledge of coun-tries other than Japan made him a popular deity with traders; and, for the same reason, he was also associated with communications. In addition to his healing skills, Sukuna-Biko was able to control and give protection against wild beasts, snakes, and insects.

He was an ally of Okunikushi, the son-in-law of the storm god Susanowo, and helped him to rule the land of Izumo on the shores of the Sea of Japan.

Sukuna-biko was of minute stature, so small that when he rested on a stalk of millet, a breath of wind flung him into space.

ALSO KNOWN AS: Sukuna-Hikona

✳

HEALING

✳

ASCLEPIUS
Greece

Asclepius, the god of healing, was the son of the sun god Apollo and Coronis, a lake nymph. While expecting Apollo's child, Coronis was unfaithful to her divine husband with a mortal. Apollo sent his sister Artemis, goddess of the hunt, to kill his adulterous wife; but, as the fire blazed on her funeral pyre, Apollo regretted his deed and snatched his son, still alive, from his mother's womb.

Asclepius was entrusted to Chiron, who was the wisest of the Centaurs and taught him the art of medicine and surgery and the secrets of healing. He was so gifted that he surpassed his master and was able to bring the dead back to life. Hades, the lord of the underworld, anxious lest he lose his subjects, complained

The main cult center of Asclepius was at Epidaurus. It was served by priests who held the art of healing exclusively from the god and transmitted it from father to son.

to Zeus. The supreme god could not allow the order of the world to be upset and killed Asclepius with a thunderbolt.

Apollo was heartbroken, but powerless against the great god. In revenge, he sought out the one-eyed Cyclopes who had fashioned the lethal thunderbolt, and slew them.

The center of the cult of Asclepius was at Epidaurus. To be cured, it was necessary first to be purified through fasting, abstinence, and refraining from sexual relations. The sick slept in the temple on bare ground that they shared with non-poisonous snakes. Asclepius visited them in their dreams and prescribed their cures or treatments.

The god was represented as a kindly, bearded old man, holding a staff round which a snake was entwined. His daughter was Hygeia, goddess of health. One of his most famous followers was Hippocrates.

The cult of Aesculapius, the Greek god's Roman equivalent, was introduced in the city in 293 BC after a plague epidemic.

HANDICRAFTS

PTAH
Egypt

The third most important deity after Amun, ruler of the air, and the sun god Re, Ptah was venerated as god of handicrafts at Memphis, the ancient capital of Egypt. He created the gods by his thought, and the earth by the power of his spoken word.

Sculptor of the world, after having created his own body he created all living beings on a potter's wheel.

His priests at Memphis were the most important in the country. His high priest, known as Great Chief of the Arts, directed architects and builders and was in charge of the construction of Ptah's great temples. One of these, at Memphis, became indirectly responsible for the country's name. Called *Hut-ka-Ptah,* meaning "house of the spirit of Ptah," it was translated as *Aiguptos* by the

Ptah's priests claimed that he made the world. By his word, he created eight gods including Atum to be his thought, and Thoth to be his tongue.

Greeks who applied the name to the whole city, and eventually to the entire land.

Ptah was the god of artists and artisans, designers, metal workers, potters, sculptors, and craftsmen. He was depicted as a man swathed like a mummy, with a shaven head or a skullcap, wearing the beard of the gods, and holding a scepter with the *ankh*, symbol of life and the creative forces of the universe. His flesh was believed to be made of gold.

One of his greater achievements was to assist the troubled pharaoh Rameses II in defeating the Assyrians by ordering hundreds of rats to creep into the enemy camp and eat their bowstrings.

IDENTIFIED WITH: Hephaistos

✳

WOODCRAFTS
✳

TANE
Oceania (Maori)

Tane was lord of the forest and all the creatures who lived in it, and of all things made from trees. He was the son of Rangi, the sky, and Papa, the earth. The primal couple embraced so tightly that their children, cramped and stifled, decided to separate them and go out into the world.

Tane alone succeeded and, because his parents were naked, proceeded to dress them. He painted his father, the sky, red; but it did not seem quite enough, so he added some stars, which were not very impressive in the daytime but looked marvelous at night. For his mother, Papa, he provided some trees. It is said that

Tane first planted them with their roots in the air; but he decided that the effect was not pleasing, and turned them so that their roots were in the earth.

All those who used wood venerated Tane, particularly canoe builders. On the night before they started cutting trees to make a canoe, the craftsmen prayed to the god and rested their axes in his temple.

Tane could not find a wife; his mother refused his advances so, at her suggestion, he made one from the sand of the island, breathing life into her until she sneezed. And so the first human being was created.

ALSO KNOWN AS: Kane

✳

SMITHS
✳

GOIBHNU
Celtic (Ireland)

The smith god of Irish mythology, Goibhnu combined his craft with magical powers that enabled him to create invincible weapons for the Tuatha Dé Danann, the gods of light and goodness, to use in their battles against the Formarians, malformed and evil deities of darkness.

He was also a master brewer, who used a gigantic bronze cauldron to make a special ale which he served at an otherworld feast known as Fled Ghobhnenn: anyone who drank the beer became immortal, untouched by illness or death.

The son of Dian Cécht, the Irish god of medicine, Goibhnu had two brothers:

Samhain and Cian, the father of Lug, god of all skills. When Balor of the Evil Eye, Lug's grandfather, attempted to kill his newborn grandson, the smith god became the infant's foster father and passed on to him his knowledge of artistry and handicraft.

ALSO KNOWN AS: Goibnu, Gobniu, Goibhniu

SMITHS

HEPHAISTOS
Greece

Hephaistos, the Greek smith god, was the son of the supreme god Zeus and his wife Hera. Lame, and apparently slow-witted, he was thrown out of Olympus by his mother, and landed in the ocean. But he was rescued

Hephaistos' smithy was believed to be under Mount Etna. The Greek vase ABOVE and the relief BELOW both show the god in his subterranean workshop exercising his skill to create precious objects.

---

by nymphs, and taken in and cared for by the people of the island of Lemnos. In his subterranean smithy, by means of fire, he used his marvelous art to fabricate precious objects such as the scepter of his father Zeus, the shield or aegis of Athena, goddess of intelligence, the suit of armor of the hero Achilles, the arrows of the love god Eros, and the chariot of Helios, the sun god. His skill made him the special patron of smiths and craftsmen who use fire in their trades.

The workshop of Hephaistos was believed to lie under Mount Etna in Sicily, a notion adopted by the Romans for their god Vulcan, the Greek god's counterpart. Vulcan, whose assistants were the one-eyed Cyclopes, protected mankind from fire: his feast, the

Volcanalia, was on August 23, during the driest time of year, and live fish were thrown into sacred flames to mollify him and prevent major conflagrations.

MERCHANTS AND TRADERS

EKCHUAH
Central America (Maya)

With his black-rimmed eyes, pendulous lower lip and long scorpion's tail, Ekchuah was one of the most striking gods of the Maya pantheon, with two quite different, and semi-conflicting, roles.

In one aspect, he was a benign god of merchants and travelers, and carried a bundle of merchandise on his back like a traveling salesman. But his other role was that of the Black War Leader—the meaning of his name—in which he appeared as a fierce and violent deity, responsible for all those who died in battle.

LITERATURE

WEN CHANG
China

Traditionally, the Great Bear constellation has been seen by the Chinese as the home of Wen Chang, the highly respected god of literature, whose name is inscribed on wall tablets in many homes. Originally a scholar who lived in the third or fourth century AD, his role as the deity of literature was fully established a thousand years later.

Always a popular deity, he had a separate shrine in many Taoist temples; a black horse, saddled and bridled, stood in front of the god's statues, attended by two servants, one of whom was deaf and the other mute. This demonstrated the mysteries of literature—its deafness to requests for explanation and

Kuei Hsing, assistant to Wen Chang, stands on a turtle or fish, and holds the writing brush used to mark examination papers.

its dumbness in its inability to let people comprehend its marvels.

His assistant, Kuei Hsing, was the deity of examinations; he was more popular still, and revered by the ambitious. In one legend he is described as a highly intelligent but hideous man, who achieved the highest marks of anyone in a civil service examination—but when the emperor saw his ugliness he refused to confirm him. In despair, Kuei Hsing threw himself into the sea, but was saved from drowning by a turtle or a fish.

MUSIC

BENTEN
Japan

The Japanese goddess of music is one of seven deities of good luck, and is also worshipped for her associations with wealth and eloquence. She wears a jeweled diadem and holds a stringed instrument in her hand. A darker side is her connection with snakes: her husband was a serpent king from the seas around Japan whose appearance so distressed her that she was reluctant to yield to him; and statues of her often feature coiled snakes, symbolic of jealousy. A diadem and a string instrument are other attributes.

Fittingly enough, Benten has a special responsibility for geishas—female companions who entertain men with conversation and music as well as dancing.

ALSO KNOWN AS: Benten-San

POETRY

BRAGI
Northern Europe

Bragi's parents were Odin and Gunnlod, a giantess whom the supreme god had seduced. Her father possessed a mead that had been made from a mixture of honey and the blood of the wise god Kvasir, and which turned anyone who drank it into a poet. Their son inherited the gift of poetry, and Odin gave him the task of welcoming warriors who had been slain in battle to the hall of Valhalla. Bragi's wife was Idun, the goddess who guarded the golden apples that ensured eternal youth for the gods.

COMMUNICATIONS

HERMES
Greece

The most accessible of all the Olympians, Hermes was god of the spoken word and the lovable master of chance. Zeus was particularly proud of his resourceful last-born who, within twenty-four hours of his arrival in the world, had succeeded in stealing one hundred heifers from his brother Apollo; inventing the lyre by stringing cow-gut to a tortoise shell he stumbled upon; inventing the flute and exchanging it for Apollo's magic wand and the skill of soothsaying; and justifying his deeds so eloquently that his father made him his personal herald.

In addition, because he was so ingenious and persuasive, Zeus allotted him the duties of the making of treaties, the promotion of commerce, and the maintenance of free rights of way for travelers on any road in the world.

Hermes was given the *caduceus*—the herald's staff with white ribbons (later represented as entwined serpents)—a round hat against the rain, and winged sandals to carry him across the skies with the speed of wind. As the divine messenger, he ran indefatigably from heaven to earth and back carrying news, helping to negotiate contracts, arranging love affairs, and often creating mischief just for the fun of it—or for the entertainment of the gods. Amusing but not frivolous, witty and quick-witted, he brought good fortune to thieves, rascals, merchants, and heroes alike.

His achievements were due to his cleverness and skills. He persuaded the nymph Calypso to release the wandering hero Odysseus from her charms; thwarted the goddess Circe's plan to change the hero into a pig; and guided Eurydice back to the underworld after she had been allowed to spend one day in the world of light with her husband Orpheus.

His best-known exploit was the liberation of Io, Zeus' lover, who was held captive by the hundred-eyed giant Argus on the orders of Zeus' jealous wife, Hera. Hermes charmed him to sleep with the sound of his flute and cut off his head. In homage to her servant, Hera scattered his eyes over the tail of the peacock, her sacred bird.

Like most other Greek gods, Hermes had innumerable lovers including goddesses, nymphs and mortals—even sheep and goats. Hermaphrodite and Pan were two of his most famous sons.

Vigorous and good-looking, the god was

Hermes was also the god of trade and commerce. From the eighth century BC, Ephesus (in modern Turkey) became an important trade and banking center, and its temple to Artemis was one of the seven wonders of the world until it was destroyed by invaders. This section of a column from Ephesus shows Hermes approaching a goddess; he holds the caduceus or herald's staff.

worshipped by athletes and credited with the invention of racing and boxing. His statue stood at the entrance of the stadium at Olympia—where the Olympic games were held—and in every gymnasium in Greece.

As the god of travelers and of fertility, his bust rested on pillars, known as *herms*, carved with impressive male organs, that were set up at every crossroad. Similar *herms* were used as garden ornaments by the Romans, and a series was designed by Nicolas Poussin for the royal gardens at Versailles.

Mercury was the Roman counterpart of Hermes and inherited his attributes. He grew in importance as the influence of astrology developed in the Middle Ages.

RIGHT *Hermes, wearing the magic winged sandals that enabled him to travel swiftly as the messenger of the gods, is shown here in his aspect as the idealized young athlete.*

BELOW *This representation of Hermes on a Greek red-figure cup, shows him with the complete panoply of the divine herald: staff, hat, and winged sandals.*

CHAPTER NINE

TRUTH, KNOWLEDGE, AND JUSTICE

WISDOM
✦

BRAHMA
India

Originally a creator god, Brahma is now associated with wisdom as the deity who has knowledge of the sacred scriptures of Hinduism, and who represents the balance between the extremes of Vishnu, who preserves the world, and Shiva the destroyer. His consort is Sarasvati, goddess of the arts.

In his role as a deity of creation, Brahma was born from a golden egg that Brahman, the cause of all existence, had grown in the cosmic waters from which the universe would be formed. After he had emerged from the egg, its two halves became heaven and earth; forming the sky between them was his first act as a creator god. Another legend describes how Brahma was born from a lotus in Vishnu's

✦

Maat, the goddess of justice, wears the ostrich feather, ideogram of her name and symbol of truth. Her role was crucial to the souls of the dead when they reached paradise.

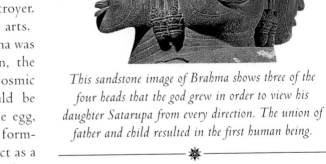

This sandstone image of Brahma shows three of the four heads that the god grew in order to view his daughter Satarupa from every direction. The union of father and child resulted in the first human being.

✦

navel in the presence of Lakshmi, the goddess of beauty and good fortune.

The god created the goddess Satarupa from his own body—a young woman so beautiful and enchanting that he grew four heads in order to watch her as she circled him to show respect. His incestuous desire overcame him and his union with his daughter produced Manu, the first human being.

Brahma has four arms as well as four heads, and in his hands he holds the four *Vedas,* the sacred writings of Hinduism. He has red skin, wears a white loincloth, and rides through the heavens on a gander.

The lifespan of the universe is calculated in terms of the god's own life: he is expected to live for a hundred celestial years, the equivalent of nearly four million years on earth. His age today is fifty-one.

TRUTH

MAAT
Egypt

Maat, the goddess of truth and justice, was the daughter of Re, the sun god, and embodied cosmic harmony. She maintained order on earth and in heaven, and ruled over the seasons, night and day, and the movement of the stars. The pharaohs, who upheld the laws of the universe, received their authority to govern from the goddess.

Her power was immense. Maat was the regulator of religious rites, and presided over decrees, legal acts, and social relationships. Her high priest was the vizier, supreme head of the tribunals. But it was in the underworld that the goddess of truth played her most important role.

There, in the hall of the two truths, Maat sat in judgment on those who had died. Their heart, or conscience, was weighed on her scales against the feather of truth, and she

alone decided on their fate. If the heart was heavy with sin and tipped the scale, the deceased was devoured by a monster, part-crocodile, part-lion, part-hippopotamus. Paradise was the reward if the scales balanced. On earth, judges were so much in awe of Maat that they always held a statuette of her in their hand when giving judgment. The goddess of truth was usually depicted wearing an ostrich feather, her symbol, in her headdress.

ALSO KNOWN AS: Mait, Ma

RETRIBUTION

NEMESIS
Greece

Nemesis, the Greek goddess of retribution, punished anyone who showed arrogance and pride, or hubris, with the greatest severity; and also had the responsibility of ensuring that luck and justice were evenly shared out. A child of the night, she was responsible with the Furies, three avenging goddesses, for transporting the souls of dead wrongdoers to Tartarus, the region of punishment in the underworld.

In one legend, the goddess was raped by Zeus and gave birth to Helen, the fabled beauty for whom heroes and kings fought and wars were waged.

Nemesis' cult was centered in Attica and Smyrna and she was represented by a winged griffin. She became a goddess of sports and, in Rome, she was honored at racetracks.

This detail from an Athenian cup shows the birth of Athena: the goddess sprang, fully grown and armed with a shield, from the head of Zeus which Hephaistos split open with an ax.

INTELLIGENCE

ATHENA
Greece

Originally the special goddess of the princes of Crete and Mycenae, Athena, as goddess of wisdom and intelligence, became one of the principal deities of the Greek pantheon. She sprang to life fully formed from the head of her father, the supreme god Zeus, after he had swallowed her mother Metis, his mistress, to protect her from the jealous wrath of his wife Hera. Hephaistos, the smith god, assisted at the birth with his ax. Always Zeus' favorite, the goddess was known to him as "Athena bright eye," and remained always a virgin (in Greek *parthenos*). Her temple at Athens, the Parthenon, was the principal center of her cult.

In her early incarnations, as a Cretan palace goddess, Athena was associated with snakes, and was sometimes described as owl-eyed and Gorgon-faced. But she was best known as Pallas Athena, a warlike yet beautiful maiden, often clad in armor, who was the patron goddess and special protector of the city of Athens. She won this privilege in a contest with the sea god Poseidon, adjudicated by Zeus, by conjuring forth an olive tree on the Acropolis where Poseidon could produce only a saltwater spring. The Palladion, a sacred image of Athena that was carefully preserved in the Parthenon, was said to protect the city from all harm.

Athena was also the goddess of battle, but unlike Ares, the god of war, she relied on intelligence rather than brute force to achieve her ends. She bore the aegis, a breastplate with the head of the Gorgon Medusa, into battle; and she supported the Greeks in their war against the Trojans, whom she hated bitterly because Paris, son of King Priam of Troy, had judged the love goddess Aphrodite to be more beautiful than either she or Hera.

The hero Odysseus was greatly helped by Athena in his long journey back from the Trojan War.

Athena was also a patron of arts and crafts. She gave people ploughs, looms, and flutes, and had a special interest in spinners and weavers. Despite being a patron of smiths, however, she resolutely refused to wed the ugly smith god Hephaistos and vanished from their bridal bed. His seed fell to the ground and produced Erichthonos, who became the first king of Athens.

The Roman goddess Minerva, protector of doctors, teachers, and craftsmen, and seen as the goddess of wisdom and the arts, came to be associated with Athena. She too developed warlike attributes as the special goddess of Rome, and was depicted wearing a helmet, shield, and coat of mail. During her festival at the end of March, the Palladian statue of her, which was said to have fallen from Mount Olympus, was carried in procession round the streets of Rome.

LEARNING

BRIGID
Celtic (Ireland)

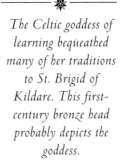

The Celtic goddess of learning bequeathed many of her traditions to St. Brigid of Kildare. This first-century bronze head probably depicts the goddess.

The Celtic goddess of poetry, wisdom, and arcane learning, Brigid's name means "Queen," "the Powerful One," or "exalted." A powerful deity—her father was the Dagda, the supreme god of Irish Celtic mythology—she was also associated with healing and fertility, and was deeply concerned to give women ease during childbirth.

Brigid had two consorts: Bres, the handsome but tyrannical son of the king of the Formarians—evil spirits who lived under the sea—whom she married; and Tuireann by whom she had three sons. Their travels, as recompense for killing the father of Lug, the god of "all skills," are the Irish equivalent of Jason's quest for the golden fleece.

Brigid was renowned for her beneficence—according to Scottish tradition it was she who deposed the blue-faced goddess of winter every spring—and also for her generosity, a characteristic she bequeathed to St. Brigid of Kildare, who lived in the fifth century, and whose extravagance in giving her family's property to the poor drove her father to distraction. The Christian saint also inherited many of the traditions associated with her pagan predecessor: she was invoked during childbirth; and her feast day, February 1, is the old festival of spring, the ancient *imbolc* that celebrated ewes coming into milk, and that was sacred to the Celtic goddess.

ALSO KNOWN AS: Brigit, Brighid

LEARNING

❋

HANUMAN

India

The god of learning, Hanuman was the son of Vayu, god of the winds, and possibly for this reason is renowned for both his speed and his ability to fly. Half human and half monkey, he leads an army of apes. He was the faithful servant and companion of Rama, an incarnation, or avatar, of the great god Vishnu, and supported him loyally in his battle with the demon Ravana.

The *Ramayama,* the epic Hindu poem that describes Ravana's abduction of Rama's wife Sita and her rescue, records that the monkey god leapt across the sea to Sri Lanka, Ravana's stronghold, but was intercepted by a female demon, Surasa, who attempted to swallow him. Hanuman first extended his body so that she was forced to elongate her mouth, then shrank to the size of a thumb and flew out of her ear. When he landed in Sri Lanka he was taken prisoner by Ravana who, rather than killing him, set fire to his tail, which the cunning monkey god used as a flaming brand to destroy the island. For this feat, and his many other services, Rama awarded him the gift of eternal life and youth.

❋

The monkey god of learning was one of the heroes of the Ramayama, Hinduism's epic poem.

KNOWLEDGE

❋

THOTH

Egypt

Credited with the invention of hieroglyphic writing, the measurement of time, and the foundation of law, Thoth was the god of knowledge and wisdom.

He was portrayed as an ibis or ibis-headed, or sometimes as a squatting baboon. In all cases, he wears a crown representing the crescent moon supporting the full moon disk—the moon is the instrument the Egyptians used to calculate time. His chief center, Dhouit (later Hermopolis), from which one of the variations of his name derives, possessed the finest library in the empire. As the secretary of the gods, he was responsible for all calculations, kept the accounts, controlled the archives, and wrote the laws and the book of magic. The inventor of writing, he imparted his secret knowledge to a few scribes who learned how to write with pictures—a form of magic—and acquired immense powers. The palette, black and red inks, and reed pen they used were the symbols of their scholarship.

Thoth's knowledge was so comprehensive that it won him his name, which means "three times great." He was the god of wisdom, magic, music, medicine, astronomy, geometry, drawing, history, chronology, language, and speech. He also invented all the arts and all the sciences, and created the calendar. On his feast day, sweets, figs, and honey were exchanged, and the traditional greeting was "Gentle is the truth!"

He was a conciliator—always good, true, and impartial. It was said that the peace of the gods was in him. But he could be ruthless with the enemies of truth: he decapitated them and cut out their hearts. As a judge in the underworld, he supervised the balance of the scales which determined the fate of the deceased.

Thoth learned to cure all wounds when he acquired the mastery of many spells, including one that ensured that love would be returned. He finally retired to the sky and became god of the moon.

ALSO KNOWN AS: Thot, Thoout, Djehuti, Dhuit

IDENTIFIED WITH: Hermes

In this Egyptian painting, Thoth is depicted as a man with the head of an ibis. He holds the symbol of the scribes over whom he presides.

LEFT Ibis-headed Thoth is portrayed here in his role as judge of the dead. His wife was the goddess Maat.

BELOW A royal scribe writes under the protection of Thoth, seen here in his baboon form. Egyptians thought that this animal represented great wisdom.

CULTURE

ITZAMNA
Central America (Maya)

Itzamna, the most revered god of the Maya pantheon, was entirely benevolent and was never associated with any human or natural disasters. His important role as the deity who brought knowledge, culture, and writing to his people is reflected in depictions of him as an enthroned king, priest, or scribe. At ceremonies in honor of the god, priests presented writings to his effigy.

Itzamna was also a sun god, and lord of the east and west, and of day and night. He was the founder of the Mayan capital, Mayapan, and named other principal places; he brought maize and cocoa to mankind, established religious ceremonies and rituals, and divided out the land.

The god was usually represented as a kindly old man with toothless jaws, sunken cheeks, and a protuberant nose. Although he was benevolent, at Chichen Itza, in the Yucatan peninsula, human sacrifices were regularly made to a gigantic statue of a crocodile which was believed to represent him, to ensure that he did not turn against the people he had so greatly benefited.

CHAPTER TEN

❋

WAR AND PEACE

WAR

❋

THE AHAYUTA ACHI
North America (Zuni)

The Ahayuta Achi were the vigorous and powerful twin gods of war of the Zuni Pueblo people of southwestern North America. The children of the sun, Yatikka Taccu, and a woman named Dripping Water, they came into being from the foam of a waterfall when it was struck by the rays of the sun. They lived with their grandmother, Spider Woman, and from an early age demonstrated unusual prowess: they made a dangerous journey to visit their father the sun, slaying many foes on the way; and later stole rain-making implements from the ferocious Saiyathlia warriors.

The twins were fiercely protective of the Zuni people, on whose behalf they destroyed

---
❋

Brigantia, the Celtic goddess of victory, was the guardian deity of a British tribe that resisted Roman rule for more than 150 years; here she holds a spear and globe of rulership.

monsters and evil-doers, and to whom they gave working tools and knowledge of hunting methods. But these brave fighters also had a mischievous side and at times encouraged gambling and trickery.

❋

WAR

❋

HUITZILOPOCHTLI
Central America (Aztec)

Huitzilopochtli, the supreme Aztec deity, sun god, and above all the god of war, was believed to have sprung fully armed from the body of his mother, the earth goddess Coatlicue at Coatepec, the Serpent Hill near Tula. She had been murdered by her sons, the four hundred stars, and her daughter, Coyolxauhqui the moon, and in revenge Huitzilopochtli killed all of them with his flaming fire serpent—day thus triumphed over night. This legend was re-enacted at the great temple at Tenochtitlan by the Aztec priests when human sacrifices were dismembered and tumbled down the temple steps. To the

Spanish armies of Hernando Cortés, when they observed this and other similar rituals, Huitzilopochtli represented the devil.

The god was depicted as a blue man with a serpent foot, wearing a blue-green headdress of hummingbird feathers, a golden tiara, white heron feathers, and holding a smoking mirror and a fire serpent. His face was striped with blue and yellow and he wore a black mask with stars round his eyes. His appearance embodied his attributes as the god of the morning and daytime, summer and the south. Many Aztecs believed him to be a young warrior who was born each day, defeated his enemies, the moon and stars of the night, and was aided in his daily death and resurrection by the souls of warriors.

But according to another tradition, the god was a semi-historical figure who played a key part in the Aztec rise to power in Central America. Originally an obscure and powerless tribe, the Aztecs were led away from their ancestral island homeland near Atzlan in northern Mexico by Huitzilopochtli to conquer the country's valley and plateau. At the outset, he addressed his fellow Aztec chiefs,

This rare representation of Huitzilopochtli—whose name translates as "left-handed hummingbird"—is from a sixteenth-century manuscript in which a Christian missionary, Bernard de Sahagun, describes the horrors of the human sacrifices that were made to appease the Aztec god of war. According to legend the god inspired his people to find, and finally settle in, what is now Mexico City.

saying that his mission was war and that it must be pursued without mercy. As the tribe moved south, Huizilopochtli, represented by a magical image, continued to inspire his people with promises that they would conquer the known world, and receive great treasures and tributes. Eventually the Aztecs stopped at Lake Texcoco, where Huitzilopochtli instructed them to rename themselves as the Mexica and to settle there; and the city of Tenochtitlan (now Mexico City)—with its sophisticated street plans and architectural splendours—was founded.

On his main feast Huitzilopochtli, in the form of a great dough figure, was offered flowers, incense, and food adorned with wreaths and garlands of flowers, then carried to the temple and eaten. But on many other festivals he received quite different tributes, gleaned from the "Flowery Wars." These were regular campaigns waged by the Aztecs against their subject tribes, with the aim of taking live captives to humiliate and weaken the enemy and to appease Huitzilopochtli, god of war.

A sixteenth-century Christian missionary, Bernard de Sahagun, described how these prisoners—men, women, and children—were sacrificed to the god. Having been dragged by their hair up the temple steps, they were killed by the priests who tore out their hearts, flayed the corpses, and dismembered their limbs. Portions of their flesh were sent to the ruler and nobility to eat, and the rest were fed to animals; the skulls were placed in ceremonial skull racks. For the Aztecs, these sacrifices were essential in order to appease the voracious appetite of Huitzilopochtli, so that he would preserve them as the proud rulers of Central America.

WAR

❋

TYR
Northern Europe

The god of war was the son of Frigga, the goddess of fertility, and the giant Hymir. The bravest of all the Norse deities, he was instrumental in capturing and binding Fenrir, the evil wolf offspring of the mischief-making Loki. The monstrous beast terrorized Asgard, the abode of the gods, and as it became ever

Tyr sacrificed his right hand in order to save his fellow deities from the the wolf Fenrir; as a result of his action the monster was magically bound and kept captive until the coming of Ragnarok.

Viking warriors who worshipped Tyr wore his image in battle. This metal mold for a helmet plaque shows him with a chained beast, probably Fenrir.

more threatening vain attempts were made to bind it. But the wolf was powerful enough to break even the strongest chain into pieces—until Odin, with the help of dwarves, fashioned a magical cord made from imperceptible things including the beard of a woman and the breath of fish.

The gods challenged the monster to prove its strength by breaking their newest invention. The wolf agreed, but on condition that one of them put his hand into its jaws to show that no magic had been involved in making the cord. Only Tyr had the courage to do this; and when Fenrir discovered that his bonds were unbreakable, and that he was doomed to be bound for eternity, he bit off the god's hand.

ALSO KNOWN AS: Tiwaz

WAR

TEUTATES
Celtic (Gaul)

Teutates was a paradoxical deity. In his fearsome aspect as the Gallic god of war, he was worshipped with savage rituals during which sacrificial victims were drowned in a lake to propitiate him. More beneficently, he was identified with the Roman god Mercury by Julius Caesar, who described him as the inventor of the arts and the god concerned with journeys, trade, and wealth. His warlike qualities were commemorated in the twelfth century: when German knights and priests formed a military order during the Third Crusade, they adapted his name to call themselves the Teutonic Knights.

WARRIORS

INDRA
India

Indra, the god of war, was the supreme deity of the Vedic pantheon and one of the most widely invoked: more than a quarter of the hymns in the *Rig Veda* are addressed to him.

The patron of warriors, he also had authority over the weather. His weapon was a thunderbolt which might have had as many as four hundred edges, and he was the god who brought rain to the parched lands of India.

He was a mighty figure with powerful arms, but his appearance was marred by his extended belly, the result of his over-indulgence in *soma*, an exhilarating and intoxicating drink made from a hallucinogenic plant. When he had drunk it he swelled in size until he filled both heaven and earth, and was able to perform the deeds for which he was famous. One of his best-known exploits was killing Vritra, the demonic serpent of drought who held the waters of the earth prisoner: the god struck the monster's back with his thunderbolt, then split its stomach and liberated the waters. Land was separated from the sea as a result, and the sun rose for the first time.

Indra also led the gods in their battles against the Asuras, primeval deities who were their sworn enemies; and he even fought against human foes on battlefields. His attendants were a troop of storm spirits who wore golden helmets and breastplates, and caused the rain to fall by splitting clouds with their battle-axes.

In his early years, as a Vedic deity, Indra was gold or red, and was portrayed on horseback or driving a chariot drawn by horses. In Hinduism, he is depicted as a white man wearing red clothes and riding an elephant.

RIGHT Indra relaxes with his attendants. The god of war was known for his love of soma, an intoxicating and hallucinogenic drink.

ABOVE Indra was one of the three great gods of early Hinduism and the most prominent deity in the hymns of the Rig Veda.

WAR

❋

MARS
Rome

Mars, god of war, was of far greater moral stature than his Greek counterpart, Ares, and as father of Romulus, founder of Rome, was held in the highest honor by the Romans, second only to the supreme god Jupiter. He was married to Venus, the goddess of sexual love and beauty, but he was also the lover of the vestal virgin Ilia—a relationship which led to her suffering the terrible

This detail from a painting by Andrea Mantegna shows Mars with his wife Venus. The god holds a spear, symbolizing his warlike nature, and Cupid is in the background.

punishment of being buried alive. His sacred shield, which had fallen from heaven, was kept by the high priest at the forum in Rome and was believed to preserve the existence of the Roman Empire; his other emblems were a spear, a woodpecker, a wolf, and a bull.

The Emperor Augustus stressed Mars' role as the avenger, to atone for the murder of his adopted father Julius Caesar and inspire the Roman people in war. In his other role as protector of fields and crops, Mars had one of the twelve months—March—dedicated to him. On March 1 sacred buildings were decorated with laurels, and on March 14 the Campus Martius in Rome was filled with spectators watching horse races in honor of the god.

❋

VIOLENCE

❋

ARES
Greece

The Greek god of war, Ares was violent, unscrupulous, amoral, cowardly, and merciless. He briefly lured the beautiful Aphrodite, goddess of love, away from her clumsy husband the smith god Hephaistos. Ares' chariot was pulled by Phobos (fear) and Deimos (terror); and he was highly regarded by the Amazons, female warriors notorious for removing their right breast to improve their performance as archers. However, he was generally disliked by gods and mortals alike.

Ares was the first god to stand trial: once for murdering a son of Poseidon; and another time for raping his own daughter.

VICTORY

✳

BRIGANTIA
Celtic (Britain)

A Celtic goddess of victory, Brigantia was, fittingly enough, the guardian of the Brigantes, a northern British tribe in what is now West Yorkshire that was powerful enough to resist the might of the Roman Empire for more than one hundred and fifty years. It is likely that she is Julius Caesar's "Celtic Minerva"—one of the local deities that he described after his invasion of Britain in 55 BC. Certainly, she is associated with the Roman goddess in Minerva's warlike aspects as well as in her role as a patron of the arts and crafts: a third-century statue shows Brigantia holding Minerva's spear and a globe of rulership, with wings of victory sprouting from her shoulders. She may also, many centuries later, have been the model for Britannia, the female warrior wearing a helmet and carrying a trident who personified the British Empire.

Although the Brigantes were eventually subdued by the Roman legionaries who marched north to build Hadrian's Wall in the second century AD, their deity was still worshipped during the Roman occupation of Britain as a nymph goddess of springs.

She was the British counterpart of the Irish Brigid who was concerned with healing and medicine. She presided over many springs, and it is probable that their waters were thought to cure the sick.

ALSO KNOWN AS: Briganta, Brigindo

✳

The seated figure on this Romano-British stone relief is probably Brigantia, the goddess of victory, who was described by the Roman emperor Julius Caesar as the "Celtic Minerva," and who shared many of the Roman deity's aspects. The standing figure may represent Fortuna, Rome's goddess of good fortune.

✳

VICTORY

✳

NIKE
Greece

The Greek goddess Nike personified victory in battle and success in athletic games and chariot races. Her statue in Delphi was dedicated by the Athenians in 480 BC after their victory at Salamis over the Persians. Depicted as a small winged messenger with a laurel wreath, girdle, and palm leaf, she often appears on vases helping to prepare soldiers for battle or athletes for their contests.

To the Romans, Nike became a symbol of victory over death while their own equivalent, Victoria, ensured victory in battle, and was as a result very popular with the Roman legionaries. In 29 BC, an altar to Victoria was dedicated in the senate house, and she often appears on Roman coins. In Christian times she came to be venerated as an angel.

Nike was a winged messenger of the gods and the goddess of victory. This relief shows her in flight.

This statue shows Nike standing in the guise of a ship's figurehead. After the coming of Christianity the Greek deity was transformed into an angel.

PEACE KEEPER

KUAN TI
China

Kuan Ti was originally a Robin Hood figure, a brave fighter, who was deified as the god of war. Born in the third century AD, he was a seller of bean curd who studied in order to better himself. He quarreled with his family and was imprisoned by them. He later escaped, but killed a magistrate while doing so, and became an outlaw. He joined forces with two companions and, as Brothers of the Peach Orchard, stole from the rich to give to the poor. He became known as one of China's finest warriors, and more than one thousand years after his death, in 1594, he was elevated to the rank of god of war—but as a protector against strife rather than as an aggressor. He was highly effective in this role, appearing in the sky in 1856 to help and support the imperial forces in battle.

The god's warlike functions have been linked with his role as a divine guardian of righteousness, a deity who protects men and women from strife and evil. He is also the patron of many trades, including bean-curd sellers and, because in his young days he had learned many sacred texts by heart, a god of literature.

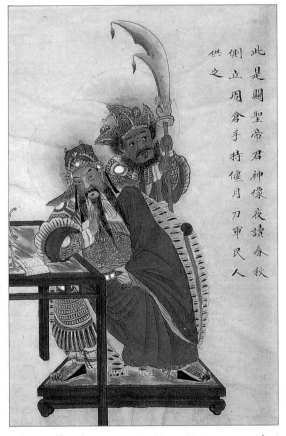

Originally a brave warrior, Kuan Ti is now a god of peacekeeping and a god of literature; a civilizing influence, he upholds justice, is able to avert conflicts, and is the patron of numerous trades.

PROTECTOR

HACHIMAN
Japan

Hachiman has both divine and human origins, and is associated with peace as much as he is with war. As a *kami*, or sacred power, he was responsible for farmers and fishermen, and was the guardian deity of the islands of Japan before becoming a god of war. He is also identified with Ojin, a third-century emperor who was renowned for his military exploits, yet encouraged immigrants from China and Korea to introduce the teachings of Confucius in order to help develop Japanese culture. Living standards improved greatly during Ojin's reign and he was later deified as Hachiman.

A sanctuary was erected on the site where the emperor had been born, and the link between ruler and deity began some centuries after Ojin's death, when a *kami* appeared to a priest in the form of a child and identified itself as Hachiman.

In the eighth century, as Shinto and Buddhist traditions grew closer, the god was styled a bodhissativa—a buddha-in-waiting.

In the past, soldiers took relics from one of his many shrines into battle with them, and today the shrines are still numerous. But although many young men celebrate their coming of age at one of them, the god's peaceful attributes now predominate over his more warlike aspects. Hachiman has returned to his original role: that of a protective deity, a protector of life and guardian of children, and a god of peace.

✳

CHAPTER ELEVEN

DARK GODS

TRICKSTER

✳

MAUI
Oceania

The legendary achievements of "Maui of the thousand tricks" range from the creation of the Polynesian islands to the gift of fire to human beings. Polynesia means "numerous islands" and it owes its existence to the great god who, with his magic fish hook, pulled up its atolls and archipelagoes from the bottom of the Pacific. The hook was his grandmother's jawbone and he had starved her to death to obtain it. Maui also caught a gigantic fish which he asked his brothers to keep for him. But it tossed and flapped so violently that they cut it in half—and created the North and South Islands of New Zealand.

The great trickster had been born prematurely and his mother, thinking he was dead,

✳

A pottery figure of Mictlantecuhtli, the Aztec lord of the underworld. As the dead traveled to his realm, a world of shadows and ice, they were reduced to skeletons by a wind of knives.

cast him out into the ocean wrapped in a tuft of hair. Rescued by the sky god, Tana, he grew up fast. He tracked down his family and, although he was unbelievably ugly, became his mother's favorite child.

Although Maui resorted to many mean tricks, he also used his cunning for good causes. He lifted the vault of heaven to give human beings more room on earth. And because he thought men and women needed a longer day in which to carry out their life tasks, he snared the sun in his fishing net and beat it until it was able just to creep along its course. To give mankind fire, Maui tricked the fire goddess, Mahui-Ike, into giving him her fingernails which contained this precious element. But when he asked for her toenails as well, she realized she had been fooled and was so angry that she set the whole world on fire. Maui called down the rain to extinguish the blaze and changed into an eagle to escape the flames; but he was scorched before he could fly away—the reason why all eagles now have brown feathers.

Maui was first the lover and then the victim of Hina, the Maori goddess of death. She had huge sexual appetites which her husband Te Tuna, a giant monster eel, no longer satisfied;

and she loudly sought a new lover. No one dared to be a candidate for fear of Te Tuna, but Maui challenged him, struck him down with his gigantic dazzling phallus and claimed his prize. The first coconut tree is said to have grown from Te Tuna's head.

Later, Maui entered Hina while she was asleep in an attempt to trick her into granting immortality to the world. But the goddess awoke and crushed the trickster deity to death. According to Hawaiian tradition, however, it was the people of Hawaii who, tired of his tricks, killed Maui. His blood made shrimp red and gave its color to the rainbow.

TRICKSTER

COYOTE
North America

The best-known figure in North American mythology, Coyote, the trickster god, appears in many different roles and guises across the length and breadth of North America, from the Arctic wastes to Mexico. Coyote the god shares, in a more extreme form, many of the attributes of coyote the animal: he is a crafty scavenger, fleet of foot, and above all a cunning and frequently malign trickster.

In the Navajo creation myth, Coyote is seen to good advantage as a hero and savior, acting as a fellow creator with First Man and First Woman, and coming up from the underground world bearing plant seeds which he gave to the different tribes as his companions fashioned them. In contrast, the Apache

blamed him for the arrival of the destructive Europeans; the creation myth of the Maidu of California shows him to be cosmically evil.

In the Maidu story, Coyote and his dog Rattlesnake emerged from the earth and watched as the world and its people were brought into being by the creator god Wonomi, helped by First Man and First Woman. Coyote tried to create people too, but laughed at the wrong moment, with the result that they had glass eyes. Angry, he lured mankind away from Wonomi and gave them sickness, sorrow, and death. His own son was the first to die from a bite by Rattlesnake, but Coyote merely laughed again.

Many stories tell of Coyote's enormous carnal appetites, which he uses his strength and trickster powers to indulge. He forces incestuous relationships on his mother-in-law, his sister-in-law, and his own daughter. He has an appetite for menstrual blood, and he often exchanges his skin with that of an unsuspecting hunter so that he can sleep with his wife. He disguises himself as a woman and transforms his male member into a baby in order to seduce young girls.

His trickster powers can also be used for more benign ends, as when he punishes a cruel and very stupid giant from a race that preys upon small and defenseless children. Coyote lures the giant into a dark cave and then pretends—by the substitution of the leg of a dead deer for his own—that he can break his own leg and then mend it by spitting on it. The giant breaks his own limb, fails to mend it no matter how hard he spits, and is left writhing in agony on the floor of the cave.

Another rich vein of Coyote stories shows the trickster tricked. Coyote chases a rabbit who escapes and bolts into his burrow.

Furious, Coyote tries to smoke him out, but the rabbit outwits him by hurling out fire and hot pitch to burn him. On another occasion, Coyote gambles against the chickadees, who are throwing their eyes into a tree, pledging his own eyes as well. The chickadees steal his eyes and replace them with hot pitch, pointing to the moral that pride goes before a fall.

In the nine-night Coyoteway healing ceremony of the Navajo, Coyote has a paradoxical role, figuring both as the divine originator of sickness and disease, and also as the means to overcome it. If someone from the tribe falls ill, through killing a coyote or even seeing one dead, part of the Coyote myth is ceremonially enacted. This enables the victim to meet with a Coyote impersonator and thus to renew his physical and spiritual balance.

Various tales are told of how Coyote met his end. In one, Coyote, having seduced a beautiful girl, Tingling Maiden, by a trick, is cruelly rejected as an equal by the hunters of her tribe and is killed by the hostile Spider People. But the higher gods take pity on him and resurrect him to new life. In another version, Coyote eventually kills himself and wanders the earth as a spirit, responsible for the finality of death.

TRICKSTER

MIMI
Australia

Aboriginal myths throughout Australia feature trickster gods who, if crossed, can wreak havoc on people. Among them are the Mimi of Arnhem Land in the Northern Territory, who inhabit gaps and cracks in the ancient escarpment. Depicted as slender, ghostly, and graceful beings in the bark paintings of this high region, they can sometimes be heard at night when they sing and beat rhythmically on the rocks where they live.

Although they are in many ways generous and helpful—they taught mankind to hunt—the Mimi have a dark side. Hunters foraging through the bush call out to announce their presence because the tricksters can visit severe illnesses on strangers who disturb them. The hunters must also take care to avoid killing or harming, even inadvertently, any wallaby that seems to be tame: it might be a pet of the Mimi who will punish anyone who injures it with death.

The figures—two male and two female—in this bark painting from Arnhem Land in Northern Australia probably represent Mimi, the trickster deities who live in the region's escarpments.

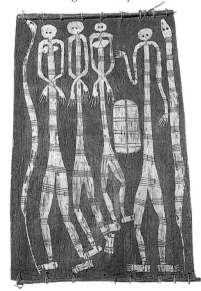

MAGIC

✸

ISIS
Egypt

The greatest goddess of ancient Egypt, Isis was the embodiment of the faithful wife and loving mother. As the divine ruler of Egypt, she introduced marriage, and taught the people to make bread, spin, weave, and cure disease.

Isis became a goddess of immense magical power by tricking the sun god Re, who had become old and senile. Mixing some of his saliva with mud, she created a poisonous snake whose bite sent Re into agonies of pain. Isis offered to cure him on condition that he reveal his secret name, which contained the power of life and death when said out loud. Re accepted her offer and recovered, and the power of Isis then surpassed that of all other gods—including the great sun god.

The daughter of the twin deities Nut and Geb, Isis married her own brother Osiris, the first king on earth. He was a good ruler who was loved by all, but he was murdered by his jealous brother Seth who, after having hidden the corpse, seized power and usurped the throne.

Isis was inconsolable. She searched the world until she found her dead husband. Hovering over him in the

ABOVE This bronze statue encrusted with gold shows Isis suckling her beloved son Horus. In her role as divine mother, she is often assimilated with the cow goddess Hathor and is shown wearing a crown of cow horns with a sun disk.

RIGHT This gold pendant shows Isis and Nephthys spreading their winged arms to protect their brother Osiris, symbolized by the central pillar, surmounted by a solar disk, and representing stability.

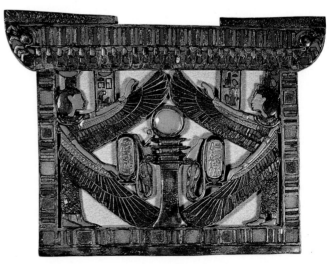

RIGHT *Isis (left) wears the headdress—the throne symbol—with which she is usually portrayed. One tradition has it that she was originally the personification of the throne, seen as a female deity.*

BELOW *The pharaoh Rameses III greets Isis on behalf of his deceased son, as the goddess visits the prince's tomb in both her roles: as ideal mother and protector of the dead.*

form of a sparrowhawk, she fanned him back to life with her wings long enough to have sexual intercourse and conceive her son, Horus. She then embalmed the body, thereby establishing rites of embalming for the future, and restored her beloved Osiris to eternal life.

Thereafter, Isis was the protector of the dead. But she devoted her life to her son, shielding him from dangers with her magic and, by her trickery, helping him to overcome the usurper Seth and avenge Osiris.

She was usually portrayed in human form, suckling the infant Horus, or with a crown of cow horns and a solar disk because of her association with the cow goddess Hathor as ideal mother. She wears a girdle bound by a *tyet,* a magic knot with life-giving power, carries a rattle or *sistrum,* and is sometimes shown protecting the dead with her winged arms. In her magnificent temple at Philae, an island in the upper reaches of the Nile, north of Aswan, stood a statue of her that bore the inscription, "I am that which is, has been, and shall be. My veil no one has lifted. The fruit I bore was the Sun."

IDENTIFIED WITH: Astarte, Aphrodite, Juno, Io

MISCHIEF-MAKING

✳

LOKI
Northern Europe

False, cunning, and occasionally sinister, Loki's handsome appearance belied his malicious character. A foster brother of Odin, and a close companion of Thor, he was nevertheless closer to the frost giants, sworn enemies of the gods, than to his fellow deities. Angrboda, his second wife, was a giantess and by her he had three monstrous offspring—Hel who was the goddess of the underworld and death, the demonic wolf Fenrir, and the Midgard serpent—who will help to overwhelm the gods at Ragnarok. Loki himself will steer the ship that carries the giants to this final battle between the forces of good and evil.

Loki was able to change his shape at will: he visited Freya, the goddess of sexual love, in the form of a flea, and became a flame and then a polar bear during a battle with Heimdall, the gods' watchman. He also appeared as a bird, a seal, and an old crone.

The trickster god could use his wiles constructively. When Idun, the goddess who guarded the golden apples of eternal youth, was kidnapped and imprisoned by the giant Thiassi, the gods, devastated by the rapid onset of age and senility, commanded that Loki rescue her. Although he had been instrumental in Idun's abduction, he agreed to do so and was successful. He flew to the giant's castle in the shape of a falcon, changed the goddess into a nut and, after a battle with Thiassi who turned himself into an eagle, returned to Asgard with her in his claws.

Loki's greatest crime was his refusal to weep for Balder and so secure the god's release from *hel*. The gods were infuriated, and to escape them he turned himself into a salmon and hid in a river. But Odin, Thor, and the wise god Kvasir caught him in a net that

✳

The trickster god of Norse mythology occasionally helped the deities of Asgard but was more often malicious and cunning. This image on a forge stone shows him with his lips sewn up as punishment for trying to cheat the dwarves who created treasures including Thor's hammer and the golden boar of Frey and Freya.

✳

This "bound devil" on a cross in northern England shows Loki in fetters after refusing to weep for Balder. He will remain bound until Ragnarok.

NECROMANCY

TEZCATLIPOCA
Central America (Aztec)

Tezcatlipoca, lord of the smoking mirror, was a supreme but dark deity worshipped in Central America from about the eighth century AD. He was believed in Toltec myth to have ruled the age of the first sun, that ended when the virtuous god Quetzalcoatl struck him down and turned him into a jaguar. But he later tempted and corrupted Quetzalcoatl and brought about his downfall. The struggle between the two deities symbolized a titanic clash between matter and spirit, good and evil.

The Aztecs adopted and adapted the cult of Tezcatlipoca. As god of the smoking mirror, he was equated with passages to the supernatural—caves, pools of water, fiery hearths, or the sun—and was patron of sorcerers and necromancy. Polished black obsidian mirrors were used by magicians in order to predict the future, and images of Tezcatlipoca show him as a serpent emerging from a mirror, or as a black skull with bands of yellow across his face—reflecting his links with the jaguar—and eyes of dark mirrors.

In his darker aspects, Tezcatlipoca was also associated with thieves and evildoers, and his female companion was Tlazolteotl, the goddess of unclean behavior. Associated with witchcraft and with the purification of sin, she acted as an intermediary between Tezcatlipoca and the penitent.

Young girls were taken from their homes in Tenochtitlan, the capital city, and formed into a corps of prostitutes in her service. On her festivals, they were sent to the military

---

he himself had woven, then bound him to three great boulders deep in an underground cavern. A snake, suspended above his head, dropped its venom onto his face and Loki's writhings at the pain this caused resulted in earthquakes throughout the world. The trickster's third wife, Sigyn, sat beside him with a bowl in which she tried to catch the drops. The mischief-maker will remain bound until Ragnarok—when he will take his revenge and, in the form of the fire serpent Sutr, reduce the world to ashes.

---

barracks to pleasure the soldiers and were then ceremonially killed.

Tezcatlipoca was also a god of kings and warriors. Capricious and all-seeing, he could hand out good fortune and wealth, but also death and misfortune, at whim to test humankind. An avenger of misdeeds, he appeared at crossroads at night to challenge soldiers to duels. He stood for the dark night sky and the north, yet also for heroes and beautiful women—in one myth he seduces Xochiquetzal, the beautiful goddess of sexual love, as the only female deity whose good looks match his own.

Each year a handsome, slim, intelligent youth, with no physical flaws, was chosen to represent Tezcatlipoca and to live as the god at Tenochtitlan. Highly honored, he was accompanied by a ceremonial retinue of eight more young men. Towards the end of the year, he was married to four beautiful girls, themselves impersonators of Xochiquetzal and other goddesses. Twenty days later, they were killed by having their hearts torn from their chests, and the cycle then began again. In this way, Tezcatlipoca was ensured a regular supply of *chalchihuatl*, the only food that the gods would accept, the essence of which was to be found in human blood alone.

DARK HOURS

HECATE
Greece

The Greek goddess of the dark hours, Hecate was also the patron of witches and a deity of necromancy, sorcery, and black magic, who lived in cemeteries, or near places where a murder had been committed. In the depths of the night, she was also found where roads met, or on pathways, accompanied by howling dogs and with snakes entwined in her hair. To meet this terrifying figure was to court disaster; offerings of food were placed at crossroads and statues were raised to her.

This mask of Tezcatlipoca, the dark god of the smoking mirror, is based on a human skull and made from turquoise and lignum. The patron of royalty and sorcerers, he demanded regular human sacrifices.

DESTRUCTION

SHIVA
India

The Hindu god of destruction owes his name to his early origins as the Vedic Rudra, "the howler" or the "terrible one," a deity so terrifying that, to propitiate him, he was later given the name Shiva or "the gracious one." In his terrible aspect he wears a necklace of skulls and a garland of serpents; he haunts cemeteries and funeral pyres, and can bedevil mankind with storms and disease. He has three eyes, one of which can destroy any living creature with a single glance; and his attendants are imps and demons.

But the god of destruction is also a god of creation, a deity who can create life as well as

Shiva the destroyer was also a creator deity, the lord of the dance who epitomized the life force. The illustration RIGHT shows him with a halo of fire, seated on a lotus and holding a drum, symbol of creation, in one of his four hands. In the statuette OPPOSITE the god is totally surrounded by flames and is dancing on a dwarf-like figure that represents ignorance.

take it. He intervened to bring the sacred river Ganges safely down from heaven to the parched earth during a prolonged drought; and, during the churning of the ocean that brought forth the sun and moon, he swallowed the poison that this generated in order to save mankind. He is the lord of the dance who, as the life force, is the source of all movement and, circled by fire, performs to relieve the sufferings of his devotees. In this

aspect, he is depicted with four arms. He holds a drum, symbolizing creation, in one hand and a tongue of flame, emblematic of destruction, in another. A third hand is outstretched in blessing and the fourth one points downwards in a gesture that promises salvation to his worshippers. He is also the arch-ascetic, the yogi who, naked and smeared with ashes, begs for his living.

Shiva bestows sexual fertility on human beings and his symbol is the *lingam*. This phallic image is said to have originated when he interrupted an argument between the great gods Vishnu and Brahma about which of them was the supreme deity by appearing as a pillar of fire—the *lingam*. Vishnu in the form of a boar tried, and failed, to find the bottom of the towering apparition. Brahma, in the shape of a gander, flew to its top where he found Shiva—the creative force of the universe and its supreme power.

The god's consorts are a reflection of his ambivalent character. Parvati, a goddess of fertility and the ultimate loving and faithful wife, is one. Another is Sati, an incarnation of Parvati, who died, grief-stricken, at her father's feet when he quarrelled with Shiva. But there is also Kali, the goddess of destruction, a terrible and malignant deity who is shown dripping with blood, with long fangs, and claw-like hands; her tongue often hangs out, and she wears a girdle of severed arms and bracelets made from snakes.

Shiva rides a white bull, Nandi, whose image is found outside his temples.

ALSO KNOWN AS: Siva

EVIL

SETH
Egypt

The son of the sky goddess Nut and the earth god Geb, and the brother of Isis, Osiris, and Nephthys, Seth was the evil deity who represented the forces of chaos. Born prematurely, he tore his mother's womb as he leapt out and, with his white skin and red hair, presented a horrible sight to Egyptian eyes.

Seth embodied fury, violence, crime, and destruction. After murdering his brother Osiris and taking the throne, he became engaged in a bloody conflict for the kingship with his nephew Horus.

Every month, he attacked the moon—the hiding place of Osiris' and his home after

Seth is depicted killing Re's arch enemy, the serpent Apophis, who tried to destroy the sun god every night during his crossing of the underworld.

death—and swallowed it. As lord of the desert, he competed with Osiris, the god of vegetation, and was responsible for drought, heat, hunger, and thirst. He destroyed crops with fire and hail. All disasters were caused by him, and his birthday was regarded as an unlucky day in the Egyptian calendar. But Seth was eventually defeated and his followers, the hated Hyksos—Semitic foreign invaders who had tried to impose his cult on Egypt— were driven out by the forces of Horus, symbol of order and good.

But the terrifying strength and violence of the evil god could be used positively. Seth had been supported by Re in his contest with

SUICIDES

IXTAB
Central America (Maya)

The Maya guardian goddess of suicides, Ixtab presided over the paradise of the blessed. She fetched all those who had committed suicide by hanging and spirited them directly to paradise. Here, joined by others who had died as soldiers in battle or as sacrificial victims, by women who had died in childbirth, and by members of the priesthood, they enjoyed a delectable existence, rewarded with delicious food and drink and resting under the shade of the pleasant tree, Yaxche, free from all want.

Ixtab's appearance depicts her function: she is portrayed as a hanged woman dangling from the sky with a noose round her neck. Her eyes are closed and her cheeks show the first signs of her decomposition.

DEATH

YAMA
India

The Hindu god of death was originally a beneficent deity who ruled over men and women who had attained an afterlife in the upper skies.

But Yama grew to be a fearsome figure: the prince of hell and judge of the dead. He wears red garments and owns a noose with which he draws out the souls from the bodies of those

Horus for the throne of Egypt; and in exchange, he successfully defended the sun god during his nightly crossing of the underworld, against his arch-enemy, Apophis, a snake god with lethal powers.

Seth was depicted as being part-pig and part-ass, with a short erect tail, long pointed ears, four long thin legs, and a curved snout. Other animals with which the god of evil was associated include the oryx, the crocodile, and the hippopotamus.

ALSO KNOWN AS: Set, Sit, Sitou, Sutekh
IDENTIFIED WITH: Typhon

who have died. His domain is bordered by a river and its entrance is guarded by two dogs, each with four eyes.

Yama is the final arbiter of the fate of the newly dead. The sentence he pronounces will decide whether their final destination is the heavenly realm over which he once reigned; whether they will return to earth to continue their journey towards salvation in the cycle of reincarnation; or whether they will be forever consigned to one of Hinduism's many hells.

Yama turns the wheel of life in this portrayal of the god of death. According to one legend he was originally a mythical king who became the first human being to die and thereby the first man to enter hell. He judges the souls who enter his domain and decides their ultimate fate.

DEATH

YEN-LO WANG
China

The Hindu ruler of the dead, Yama, came to be known in China as Yen-Lo Wang. Originally the first man to die and to find his way to the underworld, a land of ghosts, he developed into the fifth of ten terrifying judges of the dead. Although not the ultimate authority—that role was held by Ti Ts'ang Wang who delivered purified souls into their next incarnation—Yen-Lo Wang, with his nine colleagues, determined the fate of the dead in the underworld.

The passage of evildoers from this world to the place of judgment was fraught with many obstacles and trials, including lashings, attacks by savage dogs, and crossing a deep and dangerous chasm on a bridge narrower than a human foot—while righteous people crossed on bridges of silver and gold. It was at this point that Yen-Lo Wang and his colleagues decided whether each individual should have a spell in heaven or in hell, where further horrible punishments—being boiled in oil or impaled on spikes—awaited them.

Finally, Ti Ts'ang Wang dispatched the souls back to the world via the revolving wheel of the law, into a future incarnation where they might become a rich person, a poor person, or any part of the animal kingdom.

The Chinese god of death is depicted as a green demonic figure clad in the red robes of an emperor.

ALSO KNOWN AS: Yen Lo

The Chinese god of death looks down from his throne as dogs and devils chase condemned souls into the waters of a river.

DEATH

BARON SAMEDI
Haiti

The god of the dead in Voodoo mythology, Baron Samedi is a sinister and threatening figure. Dressed in a black tail coat and top hat, with dark glasses shielding his eyes, he stands at the crossroads that souls must pass on their way to Guineé, their land of origin.

As the first god to be saved from the waters of death by Legba—his West African ancestor whose cult was brought to Haiti and modified by African slaves—he is the king of the cemetery spirits, and his cross guards the grave of the first man buried in a graveyard. He is also the deity who animates the dead and turns them into zombies, bodies without souls who do the bidding of their masters.

Baron Samedi has the right to appear at ceremonies in honor of other gods or *loa* where he devours the offerings made to them. He is renowned for his love of rum and is as lecherous as he is greedy: on November 2, All Souls' Day, he takes possession of women who flock to the graveyards.

ALSO KNOWN AS: Ghede

UNDERWORLD

HEL
Northern Europe

The monstrous queen of the Norse otherworld was the third child of Loki, the mischief-making god, and the giantess Angrboda. Her siblings were Fenrir, the demonic wolf that will swallow the sun at Ragnarok; and the Midgard serpent, the monster that, on the gods' day of doom, will flood the land by lashing the sea with its tail, and overwhelm earth and sky with poisonous clouds. Hel's home was the palace of

Sleetcold, and from it she ruled men and women who had died naturally or by accident, rather than being killed in battle—lost souls imprisoned in *hel* who will fight the gods at Ragnarok. Despite her appearance—half her body was human flesh, the other was decayed—she had a lover, Ull, god of winter, who visited her for a few months each year.

UNDERWORLD

OSIRIS
Egypt

Osiris, the oldest child of the sky goddess Nut and her twin brother, the earth god Geb, was the first pharaoh. He was a good and wise ruler, loved by all, who taught his people the art of farming, weaving, and music, showed them how to make bread from grain and wine from grapes, provided laws, and spread civilization across the world—not by war but by the power of his songs.

His brother Seth, the embodiment of evil and chaos, was jealous and plotted to kill him and accede to the throne. He gave a great feast and organized a game. A beautifully decorated coffin had been secretly made to the exact measurements of Osiris; every guest was to "try it," and whoever it fitted best would win a work of art. But when Osiris lay down in it the lid was banged shut and nailed down, and the coffin was thrown into the Nile to be carried out to sea.

Isis, his loving queen and wife, was inconsolable, and had no rest until she found his body in Byblos, on the coast of Lebanon. She brought it back to Egypt and hid it in the Delta swamps. However, Seth found it and, in his fury, cut the body into several pieces which he strewed across the country. Isis found most of the pieces and used her magical powers to reconstitute her husband's body and bring him back to life.

Osiris, resurrected, began his eternal life as god of the underworld. As king of the dead, he was also their supreme judge. With the help of forty-two assessors and the record keeper, Thoth, he sorted out the good from the evil. The evil remained in the underworld; but those who were successful went to the other land, on the western horizon, where the light and warmth of the sun went at sunset; here

ABOVE Osiris, wearing the atef crown, welcomes a dead soul. Isis and ibis-headed Thoth are by his side.

OPPOSITE Ptah's dead body, flanked by Isis and Nephthys in the form of hawks, is guarded by Osiris.

LEFT *As the god of fertility and vegetation, Osiris is colored green in this wall painting. His atef crown, framed by two ostrich feathers, is the same color.*

BELOW *As in most of his representations, Osiris here wears his distinctive crown. In his crossed arms he holds the scepters of royalty—the flail and the crook.*

the souls of those who had lived good lives basked in the glory of the king of the dead.

As king of the underworld and as a fertility deity, Osiris was doubly a benefactor. He was credited with the annual rebirth and renewal of life that resulted from the flooding of the Nile which caused vegetation to sprout, and with granting eternal life and salvation.

The death and resurrection of the god symbolized the succession of the seasons and hope for another life after death.

He is depicted as a bearded mummy. His face is black or green, and he wears the narrow, plaited beard of the gods and the pharaohs, and the *atef*, a high white miter-like crown, framed by two ostrich feathers. His arms are folded across his chest, and he holds a judge's flail in one hand and the royal scepter in the other, symbols of his great powers in the underworld.

Osiris was the most beloved and venerated of all the gods, and his cult spread far beyond Egypt, to Greece and even Rome.

UNDERWORLD

EPONA
Celtic (Gaul)

Epona was the "great queen" of Celtic mythology, a powerful deity whose authority extended to the underworld but who was equally concerned with more everyday matters like healing, crops, and the fertility and use of domestic animals. Above all, however, she was associated with horses and is usually portrayed riding a mare—often

sidesaddle—and accompanied by other mares and their foals.

When the Romans defeated Vercingetorix in the final Gallic War in 45 BC, their cavalry regiments took her to their hearts and she became the only Celtic goddess known to have been worshipped in Rome.

As the "divine horse" of Celtic mythology, Epona was popular with Roman cavalry regiments.

UNDERWORLD

GWYDYON
Celtic (Wales)

Gwydyon, poet and prophet, was a sorcerer who used his magical skills in battle to win victory over his enemies. An ancient and beneficent deity, he stole otherworld pigs that belonged to the ruler of Dyfed in order to improve his people's lives. The Milky Way—the path taken by the dead—was called *Caer Gwydyon* in his honor, a reflection of his links with the underworld.

UNDERWORLD

MICTLANTECUHTLI
Central America (Aztec)

Mictlantecuhtli was the Aztec lord of the realm of the dead, and the god of the underworld, *mictlan*, where he reigned with his wife Mictecacihuatl. To this shadowy world

Mictlantecuhtli was generally depicted as a skeleton spattered with spots of blood and with the head of a skull, and was often shown wearing a collar made from eyeballs. He was placated with gifts of flayed human skin.

---

where icy cold reigned, came those who had not earned a place in the heavens, to eke out their existence on poisonous snakes, the only food. When someone died of natural causes, his or her body was dressed in fine clothes, placed on a funeral pyre with a packet of food and a red dog that had been ceremonially slaughtered, and burnt after three days, before passing on to *mictlan*.

The god's appearance made his role clear: he was depicted as a skeleton of bleached white bones with the protruding teeth of a skull and red bloody spots. Often festooned with owl

This sculpture of Mictlantecuhtli was found in Teotihuacan, the center of the Toltec religion, and shows the god's skeletal features. The Aztecs adopted his cult from the Toltecs.

feathers and head ornaments of paper, he wore a collar of eyeballs.

Gifts to the underworld god took the form of flayed human skins, and during his feast at Tlalxicco temple, believed to be the navel of the world, a man acting as his impersonator was sacrificed at night.

✳

UNDERWORLD

✳

HADES
Greece

Hades, the Greek god of the underworld, was so terrifying that people avoided speaking his name out loud and averted their eyes when making a sacrifice to him. He came into possession of his domain after the overthrow of his father, the Titan, Cronos, by the supreme god Zeus, and the division of the universe. Zeus took the heavens, and the god Poseidon the sea.

Hades became the supreme god of the underworld, a dark place inhabited by many multitudes of the dead, with the River Styx as its boundary and Charon the ferryman waiting to transport those who had died across it. The souls favored by the gods went to Elysium, the land of the blessed, and evildoers who had offended the gods were sent to Tartarus and an eternity of torture. The house of Hades was guarded by the many-headed hound, Cerberus, and no one was allowed to leave except Persephone, wife of Hades, who lived on earth for half the year. But he was not an evil deity: rather, he meted out grim but just punishments to wrongdoers. A dark-bearded god who carried a scepter and a key, he rode in a black chariot drawn by four black horses.

Two Roman gods were connected with Hades: Pluto and Orcus. Pluto—who was directly modeled on the Greek Hades—stole Proserpina, the daughter of the goddess Ceres, to be his queen and rule over the underworld with him. The Romans believed that its entrance lay at Avernus, later the site of the Christian church of Sta Maria del Inferno. The Romans also equated Hades with Orcus, a warrior god who brought fleeing cowards to book and who struck down brave fighters in their tracks. Orcus was popularly depicted as a devilish figure, a demon with black wings.

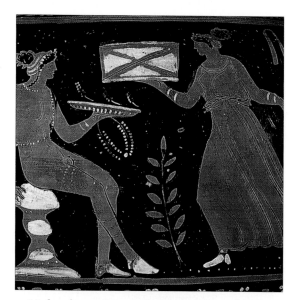

Hades, the terrifying and grim but just god of the underworld, received his domain when Zeus, his brother, overthrew their father Cronos. This detail from an amphora shows him with his wife Persephone, daughter of Demeter. No mortal who entered his realm was allowed to leave.

✳

This medieval manuscript shows Hades and Persephone seated on a
throne in the form of an eagle's head. They are guarded by Cerberus,
the many-headed hound of hell; on the right, demons torment one of
the souls doomed to spend eternity in the underworld.

INDEX OF GODS AND GODDESSES

The gods and goddesses featured in this volume are listed here in alphabetical order for easier and quicker reference.
Page numbers refer only to main entries for each deity. Names of gods and goddesses are also included in the main index.

INDEX OF RESPONSIBILITIES

Alphabetical list of responsibilities—and their gods and goddesses—mentioned in this book.
*Page numbers in **bold** indicate the main entry for a deity's responsibility.*

BIBLIOGRAPHY

Barber, R. *A Companion to World Mythology.* Harmondsworth: Kestrel Books, 1979

Burland, C. A. *Feathered Serpent and Smoking Mirror: The Aztec Gods and Fate in Ancient Mexico.* London: Orbis Books, 1980

Burland, C. A. and M. Wood. *North American Indian Mythology.* London: Newnes, 1985

Carlyon, R. *A Guide to the Gods.* London: Heinemann, 1981

Cavendish, R., ed. *Man, Myth and Magic.* London: Purnell, 1970–2

Chamberlain, J. *Chinese Gods.** Hong Kong: Long Island Books, 1983

Christie, A. C. *Chinese Mythology.* revised edn, Feltham: Newnes, 1983

Coe, M. D., E. P. Benson and D. Snow. *Atlas of Ancient America.* Oxford: Facts on File, 1985

Comte, F. *Mythology.* Edinburgh: Chambers, 1993

Cooper, J. C. ed. *Brewer's Book of Myth and Legend.* London: Cassell, 1992

Cotterell, A. *A Dictionary of World Mythology.** Oxford: Oxford University Press, 1986

Ellis, P. B. *Dictionary of Celtic Mythology.* London: Constable, 1992

Gill, S. D. and I. F. Sullivan. *Dictionary of Native American Mythology.* New York: Oxford University Press, 1992 *

Goring, R. ed. *Larousse Dictionary of Beliefs and Religions.* Edinburgh: Larousse, 1994

Grant, J. *An Introduction to Viking Mythology.* London: Apple, 1995

Graves, R. *The Greek Myths.* London: Penguin, 1992

Haile, B. and K. W. Luckert. *Navajo Coyote Tales.* Lincoln: University of Nebraska, 1984

Hart, G. *A Dictionary of Egyptian Gods and Goddesses.** London: Routledge and Kegan Paul, 1993

Hemming, J. *The Conquest of the Incas.* London: Macmillan, 1970

Jordan, M. *Encyclopedia of the Gods.* London: Kyle Cathie, 1992

Lurker, M. *Dictionary of Gods and Goddesses, Devils and Demons.** London: Routledge and Kegan Paul, 1987

Marriott, A. and C. K. Rachlin. *Plains Indian Mythology.* New York: Crowell, 1975

Miller, M. and C. Taube. *The Gods and Symbols of Ancient Mexico and the Maya: an Illustrated Dictionary of Mesoamerican Religion.** London: Thames and Hudson, 1993

Parrinder, G. *Asian Religions.** London: Sheldon Press, 1975

Radice, B. *Who's Who in the Ancient World.** Harmondsworth: Penguin, 1973

Reichard, G. A. *Navajo Medicine Man Sandpaintings.* London: Constable, 1977

Walters, D. *Chinese Mythology: an Encyclopaedia of Myth and Legend.** London: Aquarian, 1992

Willis, R. ed. *World Mythology: The Illustrated Guide.** London: Simon and Schuster, 1993

* The spellings of the names of the gods and goddesses in this book are drawn from the asterisked volumes in the list above.

INDEX

Note: Responsibilities will be found in the Index of Responsibilites.
Page numbers in italics refer to illustrations.

Volcanalia 130
Voodoo *90*, 167
Vritra 147
Vulcan 129

W
Wakan Tanka 27
Wales 170–1
water pot 74, 118
Water Sprinkler 68
Wen Chang 130–1
wheel 119, 166, *166*
Whiteshell Woman 65
willow branch *109*, 110
Woden *see* Odin

wolf 60, 148
Wonomi 154
Wotan *see* Odin
wreath 115, *116*, 149
writing 139, 140, 141
Wuotan *see* Odin

X
Xipe Totec 28, 89–90
Xochiquetzal 101, *101*, 161

Y
Yama 20, 40, 165–6, 166
Yambe *see* Nzambi
Yamuna 40

Yatikka Taccu 143
Yaxche 165
Yei 69
Yen-Lo Wang 166, *167*
Yggdrasil 24
Yin 120
Ymir 24
Yomi 14
Yoruba 15
Yu Huang Shang Ti *see* Shang Di
Yukon 61

Z
Zaire 9, 38, 65

Zambi *see* Nzambi
Zambia 65–6
zephyrs 102, *103*
Zeus 8, 16–19, *16, 17, 18, 19*, 32, 33, 38, 48, 53, 64, 73, 78, 81, 88, 89, 91, 96, 102, 105, 106, 107, 120, 127, 129, 131–2, 136, 137, 172
Zimbabwe 65–6
zombies 167
Zulus 9, 13
Zuni Pueblo 143

ACKNOWLEDGMENTS

PICTURE CREDITS
T=TOP B=BELOW C=CENTER L=LEFT R= RIGHT

Bibliothèque Nationale/Bridgeman Art Library 28B, 36B, 173; The Bridgeman Art Library 118T, 118B, 166; The British Library/Bridgeman Art Library 62, 99T; The British Museum/Bridgeman Art Library 39T, 40, 141L; The British Museum/Michael Holford 11, 31T, 42T, 69, 92TL, 92TR, 96L, 96R, 104TL, 116L; J. C. Callow/Panos Pictures 65; Chatsworth House, Derbyshire/Bridgeman Art Library 51; Chiswick House, London/Bridgeman Art Library 84; Dr Stephen Coyne/Bruce Coleman Ltd 103T; Dominique Darbois/Edimages 43T, 43B, 53, 72T, 106, 156B; Delhi National Museum/Bridgeman Art Library 147T; Delhi National Museum/Werner Forman Archive 74; C. M. Dixon 18T, 23, 32, 60R, 85, 87TL, 93B, 102T, 115, 116R, 129L, 134, 142, 149, 165, 170; Dinodia/Trip 147B; M. Dubin/Trip 80B, 106; Durham University, The Oriental Museum/Bridgeman Art Library 123; Edimages 78T, 78B, 81, 150R; Ephesus Museum, Turkey/Bridgeman Art Library 16T; ET Archive 41R, 45, 67T, 89, 122, 158; Eygptian National Museum, Cairo/Bridgeman Art Library 168; The Fitzwilliam Museum, University of Cambridge/Bridgeman Art Library 73; Christer Fredriksson/Bruce Coleman Ltd 114; Peter Furst 30B, 55, 61R, 68B, 83T, 101, 144, 171TR; Galleria Dell Accademia, Venice/Bridgeman Art Library 102B; Gemaldegalerie Kunsthistorisches Museum, Vienna/Bridgeman Art Library 75B; Giraudon/Bridgeman Art Library 103B, 133B, 148; P. Goldman Collection/Werner Forman Archive 108T, 108B; G. Gunnarsson/Trip 18B; Ben Heller Collection/Werner Forman Archive 90; Hermitage, St Petersburg/Bridgeman Art Library 63; Michael Holford 12, 20T, 20B, 21T, 28T, 44, 54B, 56, 64, 80T, 86, 88, 95, 98B, 100, 105, 113, 127B, 129R, 135, 137, 151, 161, 167, 169B, 172; The Hutchison Library 30T, 31B, 33, 39B; W. Jacobs/Trip 48T; The Louvre, Paris/Bridgeman Art Library 70T, 79, 104TR, 141R, 156T; The Mansell Collection 46, 119, 124, 133T, 150L; D. Maybury/Trip 72B; M. McKaughan/Trip 127L; The Museum of Mankind 77; National Archaeological Museum, Athens/Bridgeman Art Library 16BR; National Gallery, Prague/Werner Forman Archive 21B; National Museum, Copenhagen/Werner Forman Archive 58T, 93T; Edward Parker/Hutchinson Library 121; Collection of the Earl of Pembroke, Wilton/Bridgeman Art Library 7; Rafael Valls Gallery, London/Bridgeman Art Library 75T; Réunion des Musées Nationaux 15, 57T, 57B, 82, 110, 120; C. Rennie/Trip 37; Peter Robinson/Trip 70B; Helene Rogers/Trip 17T, 19, 48B, 49, 50, 98T, 104B, 107, 112, 139, 163; Royal Library, Copenhagen/Bridgeman Art Library 25, 59, 145; Mick Sharp 125; Historisk Museum of Stockholm/ET Archive 24; Trip 68T, 87B; Victoria & Albert Museum/Bridgeman Art Library 10, 17B, 94, 99B, 111L, 162; Victoria & Albert Museum/ET Archive 22; Viking Ship Museum, Bygdoy/Werner Forman Archive 60L; The Charles Walker Collection/Images Colour Library 26, 29L, 29R, 34, 67B, 97, 109, 111R, 140, 157T, 169TR, 171BL; The Werner Forman Archive 14, 16BL, 36T, 41L, 42B, 54T, 58BL, 58BR, 61L, 83B, 87TR, 91, 117, 130, 132, 138, 146, 152, 155, 157B, 159, 160, 164, 169TL; The Christopher Wood Gallery, London/Bridgeman Art Library 47.

EDDISON·SADD
Editors Elizabeth Hallam, Tessa Clark, and Cecilia Walters
Editorial Assistant Sophie Bevan
Proof Reader Marilyn Inglis
Indexer Dorothy Frame
Designer Lynne Ross
Picture Researcher Liz Eddison
Production Hazel Kirkman and Charles James